Mometrix
TEST PREPARATION

STAAR
Test Prep Guide
Grade 3 Reading
Language Arts

Dear Future Exam Success Story

First of all, **THANK YOU** for purchasing Mometrix study materials!

Second, congratulations! You are one of the few determined test-takers who are committed to doing whatever it takes to excel on your exam. **You have come to the right place.** We developed these study materials with one goal in mind: to deliver you the information you need in a format that's concise and easy to use.

In addition to optimizing your guide for the content of the test, we've outlined our recommended steps for breaking down the preparation process into small, attainable goals so you can make sure you stay on track.

We've also analyzed the entire test-taking process, identifying the most common pitfalls and showing how you can overcome them and be ready for any curveball the test throws you.

Standardized testing is one of the biggest obstacles on your road to success, which only increases the importance of doing well in the high-pressure, high-stakes environment of test day. Your results on this test could have a significant impact on your future, and this guide provides the information and practical advice to help you achieve your full potential on test day.

Your success is our success

We would love to hear from you! If you would like to share the story of your exam success or if you have any questions or comments in regard to our products, please contact us at **800-673-8175** or **support@mometrix.com**.

Thanks again for your business and we wish you continued success!

Sincerely,
The Mometrix Test Preparation Team

Written and edited by the Mometrix Exam Secrets Test Prep Team
Printed in the United States of America

TABLE OF CONTENTS

Introduction

Thank you for purchasing this resource! You have made the choice to prepare yourself for a test that could have a huge impact on your future, and this guide is designed to help you be fully ready for test day. Obviously, it's important to have a solid understanding of the test material, but you also need to be prepared for the unique environment and stressors of the test, so that you can perform to the best of your abilities.

For this purpose, the first section that appears in this guide is the **Success Strategies**. We've devoted countless hours to meticulously researching what works and what doesn't, and we've boiled down our findings to the four most impactful steps you can take to improve your performance on the test. We start at the beginning with study planning and move through the preparation process, all the way to the testing strategies that will help you get the most out of what you know when you're finally sitting in front of the test.

We recommend that you start preparing for your test as far in advance as possible. However, if you've bought this guide as a last-minute study resource and only have a few days before your test, we recommend that you skip over the first two Success Strategies since they address a long-term study plan.

If you struggle with **test anxiety**, we strongly encourage you to check out our recommendations for how you can overcome it. Test anxiety is a formidable foe, but it can be beaten, and we want to make sure you have the tools you need to defeat it.

Strategy #1 – Plan Big, Study Small

There's a lot riding on your performance. If you want to ace this test, you're going to need to keep your skills sharp and the material fresh in your mind. You need a plan that lets you review everything you need to know while still fitting in your schedule. We'll break this strategy down into three categories.

Information Organization

Start with the information you already have: the official test outline. From this, you can make a complete list of all the concepts you need to cover before the test. Organize these concepts into groups that can be studied together, and create a list of any related vocabulary you need to learn so you can brush up on any difficult terms. You'll want to keep this vocabulary list handy once you actually start studying since you may need to add to it along the way.

Time Management

Once you have your set of study concepts, decide how to spread them out over the time you have left before the test. Break your study plan into small, clear goals so you have a manageable task for each day and know exactly what you're doing. Then just focus on one small step at a time. When you manage your time this way, you don't need to spend hours at a time studying. Studying a small block of content for a short period each day helps you retain information better and avoid stressing over how much you have left to do. You can relax knowing that you have a plan to cover everything in time. In order for this strategy to be effective though, you have to start studying early and stick to your schedule. Avoid the exhaustion and futility that comes from last-minute cramming!

Study Environment

The environment you study in has a big impact on your learning. Studying in a coffee shop, while probably more enjoyable, is not likely to be as fruitful as studying in a quiet room. It's important to keep distractions to a minimum. You're only planning to study for a short block of time, so make the most of it. Don't pause to check your phone or get up to find a snack. It's also important to **avoid multitasking**. Research has consistently shown that multitasking will make your studying dramatically less effective. Your study area should also be comfortable and well-lit so you don't have the distraction of straining your eyes or sitting on an uncomfortable chair.

The time of day you study is also important. You want to be rested and alert. Don't wait until just before bedtime. Study when you'll be most likely to comprehend and remember. Even better, if you know what time of day your test will be, set that time aside for study. That way your brain will be used to working on that subject at that specific time and you'll have a better chance of recalling information.

Finally, it can be helpful to team up with others who are studying for the same test. Your actual studying should be done in as isolated an environment as possible, but the work of organizing the information and setting up the study plan can be divided up. In between study sessions, you can discuss with your teammates the concepts that you're all studying and quiz each other on the details. Just be sure that your teammates are as serious about the test as you are. If you find that your study time is being replaced with social time, you might need to find a new team.

Strategy #2 – Make Your Studying Count

You're devoting a lot of time and effort to preparing for this test, so you want to be absolutely certain it will pay off. This means doing more than just reading the content and hoping you can remember it on test day. It's important to make every minute of study count. There are two main areas you can focus on to make your studying count.

Retention

It doesn't matter how much time you study if you can't remember the material. You need to make sure you are retaining the concepts. To check your retention of the information you're learning, try recalling it at later times with minimal prompting. Try carrying around flashcards and glance at one or two from time to time or ask a friend who's also studying for the test to quiz you.

To enhance your retention, look for ways to put the information into practice so that you can apply it rather than simply recalling it. If you're using the information in practical ways, it will be much easier to remember. Similarly, it helps to solidify a concept in your mind if you're not only reading it to yourself but also explaining it to someone else. Ask a friend to let you teach them about a concept you're a little shaky on (or speak aloud to an imaginary audience if necessary). As you try to summarize, define, give examples, and answer your friend's questions, you'll understand the concepts better and they will stay with you longer. Finally, step back for a big picture view and ask yourself how each piece of information fits with the whole subject. When you link the different concepts together and see them working together as a whole, it's easier to remember the individual components.

Finally, practice showing your work on any multi-step problems, even if you're just studying. Writing out each step you take to solve a problem will help solidify the process in your mind, and you'll be more likely to remember it during the test.

Modality

Modality simply refers to the means or method by which you study. Choosing a study modality that fits your own individual learning style is crucial. No two people learn best in exactly the same way, so it's important to know your strengths and use them to your advantage.

For example, if you learn best by visualization, focus on visualizing a concept in your mind and draw an image or a diagram. Try color-coding your notes, illustrating them, or creating symbols that will trigger your mind to recall a learned concept. If you learn best by hearing or discussing information, find a study partner who learns the same way or read aloud to yourself. Think about how to put the information in your own words. Imagine that you are giving a lecture on the topic and record yourself so you can listen to it later.

For any learning style, flashcards can be helpful. Organize the information so you can take advantage of spare moments to review. Underline key words or phrases. Use different colors for different categories. Mnemonic devices (such as creating a short list in which every item starts with the same letter) can also help with retention. Find what works best for you and use it to store the information in your mind most effectively and easily.

Strategy #3 – Practice the Right Way

Your success on test day depends not only on how many hours you put into preparing, but also on whether you prepared the right way. It's good to check along the way to see if your studying is paying off. One of the most effective ways to do this is by taking practice tests to evaluate your progress. Practice tests are useful because they show exactly where you need to improve. Every time you take a practice test, pay special attention to these three groups of questions:

- The questions you got wrong
- The questions you had to guess on, even if you guessed right
- The questions you found difficult or slow to work through

This will show you exactly what your weak areas are, and where you need to devote more study time. Ask yourself why each of these questions gave you trouble. Was it because you didn't understand the material? Was it because you didn't remember the vocabulary? Do you need more repetitions on this type of question to build speed and confidence? Dig into those questions and figure out how you can strengthen your weak areas as you go back to review the material.

Additionally, many practice tests have a section explaining the answer choices. It can be tempting to read the explanation and think that you now have a good understanding of the concept. However, an explanation likely only covers part of the question's broader context. Even if the explanation makes perfect sense, **go back and investigate** every concept related to the question until you're positive you have a thorough understanding.

As you go along, keep in mind that the practice test is just that: practice. Memorizing these questions and answers will not be very helpful on the actual test because it is unlikely to have any of the same exact questions. If you only know the right answers to the sample questions, you won't be prepared for the real thing. **Study the concepts** until you understand them fully, and then you'll be able to answer any question that shows up on the test.

It's important to wait on the practice tests until you're ready. If you take a test on your first day of study, you may be overwhelmed by the amount of material covered and how much you need to learn. Work up to it gradually.

On test day, you'll need to be prepared for answering questions, managing your time, and using the test-taking strategies you've learned. It's a lot to balance, like a mental marathon that will have a big impact on your future. Like training for a marathon, you'll need to start slowly and work your way up. When test day arrives, you'll be ready.

Start with the strategies you've read in the first two Success Strategies—plan your course and study in the way that works best for you. If you have time, consider using multiple study resources to get different approaches to the same concepts. It can be helpful to see difficult concepts from more than one angle. Then find a good source for practice tests. Many times, the test website will suggest potential study resources or provide sample tests.

Test-Taking Strategies

This section contains a list of test-taking strategies that you may find helpful as you work through the test. By taking what you know and applying logical thought, you can maximize your chances of answering any question correctly!

It is very important to realize that every question is different and every person is different: no single strategy will work on every question, and no single strategy will work for every person. That's why we've included all of them here, so you can try them out and determine which ones work best for different types of questions and which ones work best for you.

Question Strategies

✓ Read Carefully

Read the question and the answer choices carefully. Don't miss the question because you misread the terms. You have plenty of time to read each question thoroughly and make sure you understand what is being asked. Yet a happy medium must be attained, so don't waste too much time. You must read carefully and efficiently.

✓ Contextual Clues

Look for contextual clues. If the question includes a word you are not familiar with, look at the immediate context for some indication of what the word might mean. Contextual clues can often give you all the information you need to decipher the meaning of an unfamiliar word. Even if you can't determine the meaning, you may be able to narrow down the possibilities enough to make a solid guess at the answer to the question.

✓ Prefixes

If you're having trouble with a word in the question or answer choices, try dissecting it. Take advantage of every clue that the word might include. Prefixes can be a huge help. Usually, they allow you to determine a basic meaning. *Pre-* means before, *post-* means after, *pro-* is positive, *de-* is negative. From prefixes, you can get an idea of the general meaning of the word and try to put it into context.

✓ Hedge Words

Watch out for critical hedge words, such as *likely, may, can, often, almost, mostly, usually, generally, rarely,* and *sometimes.* Question writers insert these hedge phrases to cover every possibility. Often an answer choice will be wrong simply because it leaves no room for exception. Be on guard for answer choices that have definitive words such as *exactly* and *always.*

✓ Switchback Words

Stay alert for *switchbacks.* These are the words and phrases frequently used to alert you to shifts in thought. The most common switchback words are *but, although,* and *however.* Others include *nevertheless, on the other hand, even though, while, in spite of, despite,* and *regardless of.* Switchback words are important to catch because they can change the direction of the question or an answer choice.

✓ FACE VALUE

When in doubt, use common sense. Accept the situation in the problem at face value. Don't read too much into it. These problems will not require you to make wild assumptions. If you have to go beyond creativity and warp time or space in order to have an answer choice fit the question, then you should move on and consider the other answer choices. These are normal problems rooted in reality. The applicable relationship or explanation may not be readily apparent, but it is there for you to figure out. Use your common sense to interpret anything that isn't clear.

Answer Choice Strategies

✓ ANSWER SELECTION

The most thorough way to pick an answer choice is to identify and eliminate wrong answers until only one is left, then confirm it is the correct answer. Sometimes an answer choice may immediately seem right, but be careful. The test writers will usually put more than one reasonable answer choice on each question, so take a second to read all of them and make sure that the other choices are not equally obvious. As long as you have time left, it is better to read every answer choice than to pick the first one that looks right without checking the others.

✓ ANSWER CHOICE FAMILIES

An answer choice family consists of two (in rare cases, three) answer choices that are very similar in construction and cannot all be true at the same time. If you see two answer choices that are direct opposites or parallels, one of them is usually the correct answer. For instance, if one answer choice says that quantity *x* increases and another either says that quantity *x* decreases (opposite) or says that quantity *y* increases (parallel), then those answer choices would fall into the same family. An answer choice that doesn't match the construction of the answer choice family is more likely to be incorrect. Most questions will not have answer choice families, but when they do appear, you should be prepared to recognize them.

✓ ELIMINATE ANSWERS

Eliminate answer choices as soon as you realize they are wrong, but make sure you consider all possibilities. If you are eliminating answer choices and realize that the last one you are left with is also wrong, don't panic. Start over and consider each choice again. There may be something you missed the first time that you will realize on the second pass.

✓ AVOID FACT TRAPS

Don't be distracted by an answer choice that is factually true but doesn't answer the question. You are looking for the choice that answers the question. Stay focused on what the question is asking for so you don't accidentally pick an answer that is true but incorrect. Always go back to the question and make sure the answer choice you've selected actually answers the question and is not merely a true statement.

✓ EXTREME STATEMENTS

In general, you should avoid answers that put forth extreme actions as standard practice or proclaim controversial ideas as established fact. An answer choice that states the "process should be used in certain situations, if..." is much more likely to be correct than one that states the "process should be discontinued completely." The first is a calm rational statement and doesn't even make a definitive, uncompromising stance, using a hedge word *if* to provide wiggle room, whereas the second choice is far more extreme.

⊘ Benchmark

As you read through the answer choices and you come across one that seems to answer the question well, mentally select that answer choice. This is not your final answer, but it's the one that will help you evaluate the other answer choices. The one that you selected is your benchmark or standard for judging each of the other answer choices. Every other answer choice must be compared to your benchmark. That choice is correct until proven otherwise by another answer choice beating it. If you find a better answer, then that one becomes your new benchmark. Once you've decided that no other choice answers the question as well as your benchmark, you have your final answer.

⊘ Predict the Answer

Before you even start looking at the answer choices, it is often best to try to predict the answer. When you come up with the answer on your own, it is easier to avoid distractions and traps because you will know exactly what to look for. The right answer choice is unlikely to be word-for-word what you came up with, but it should be a close match. Even if you are confident that you have the right answer, you should still take the time to read each option before moving on.

General Strategies

⊘ Tough Questions

If you are stumped on a problem or it appears too hard or too difficult, don't waste time. Move on! Remember though, if you can quickly check for obviously incorrect answer choices, your chances of guessing correctly are greatly improved. Before you completely give up, at least try to knock out a couple of possible answers. Eliminate what you can and then guess at the remaining answer choices before moving on.

⊘ Check Your Work

Since you will probably not know every term listed and the answer to every question, it is important that you get credit for the ones that you do know. Don't miss any questions through careless mistakes. If at all possible, try to take a second to look back over your answer selection and make sure you've selected the correct answer choice and haven't made a costly careless mistake (such as marking an answer choice that you didn't mean to mark). This quick double check should more than pay for itself in caught mistakes for the time it costs.

⊘ Don't Rush

It is very easy to make errors when you are in a hurry. Maintaining a fast pace in answering questions is pointless if it makes you miss questions that you would have gotten right otherwise. Test writers like to include distracting information and wrong answers that seem right. Taking a little extra time to avoid careless mistakes can make all the difference in your test score. Find a pace that allows you to be confident in the answers that you select.

⊘ Keep Moving

Panicking will not help you pass the test, so do your best to stay calm and keep moving. Taking deep breaths and going through the answer elimination steps you practiced can help to break through a stress barrier and keep your pace.

Final Notes

The combination of a solid foundation of content knowledge and the confidence that comes from practicing your plan for applying that knowledge is the key to maximizing your performance on test day. As your foundation of content knowledge is built up and strengthened, you'll find that the strategies included in this chapter become more and more effective in helping you quickly sift through the distractions and traps of the test to isolate the correct answer.

Now that you're preparing to move forward into the test content chapters of this book, be sure to keep your goal in mind. As you read, think about how you will be able to apply this information on the test. If you've already seen sample questions for the test and you have an idea of the question format and style, try to come up with questions of your own that you can answer based on what you're reading. This will give you valuable practice applying your knowledge in the same ways you can expect to on test day.

Good luck and good studying!

Reading

Vocabulary

Dictionary

A print or digital dictionary can be used to find out many things about a word. A dictionary will show the correct pronunciation of a word, provide its meaning, and identify what part of speech the word is. It will also tell how the word was derived—that is, what words it came from originally. A dictionary will have a **pronunciation guide** for each word that shows how to sound it out and where its syllables start and end. It will use symbols to indicate sounds, and will also use sample sounds (the "a" in "bad," for instance). A dictionary lists all of the meanings of a word and the parts of speech the word can be used as.

example \ ig-'zam-pəl\ noun

1. something that shows what a group of things is like
2. a model that should be either copied or avoided
3. a punishment meant to serve as a warning to others

Example:

Julia used her dictionary to check the various meanings of the word *clear*. She found this entry:

clear (klîr) adjective

1. obvious.
2. easily seen through
3. free from flaw or blemish
4. free from guilt; untroubled
5. out of the way
6. to tidy *v*
7. to free *v*
8. to earn *v*

Identify which definition of *clear* is used in the following sentence:

> Janet stood *clear* of the crowd pushing to get through the door.

The correct answer is meaning 5: "out of the way." If you substitute that definition for the word, the sentence makes sense. Meanings 1, 2, 3, and 4 do not fit with the context of the sentence. Meanings 6, 7, and 8 are verbs and "clear" as it is used in the sample is an adjective. When considering which meaning is being used, always check for context clues in the sentence or in the sentences before or after the sentence in which the word is used.

Thesaurus

A thesaurus is a reference book that gives **synonyms** of words. It is different from a dictionary because a thesaurus does not give definitions. A thesaurus can be helpful in finding the meaning of an unfamiliar word when reading. If the meaning of a synonym is known, then the meaning of the unfamiliar word will be known. Another time in which a thesaurus can be helpful is when writing. Using a thesaurus helps authors to vary their word choice.

GLOSSARY

A glossary is a **list of terms and their definitions** that can be found **at the back** of certain types of books, such as textbooks or reference books. A glossary does not have the definitions of all words, like a dictionary, but instead gives the definitions of the important terms within that particular book which are either uncommon or newly introduced. One may use a glossary when reading a book about economics or a chapter in a science textbook, for example, to define some of the technical terms within the text.

USING CONTEXT TO DETERMINE THE MEANINGS OF WORDS

Readers of all levels will encounter words that they have either never seen or that they have seen before but still don't know what it means. The best way to define a word in **context** is to look for nearby words that can assist in learning the meaning of the word.

CONTEXT CLUES

Context clues are hints about the meaning of a word. They are the words or phrases in the sentence or sentences before and after a new or unfamiliar word. Context clues give the reader an idea about what a word means. A context clue may also contain words that help define the new word or an example of what the new word means. sing context clues to figure out meaning can be helpful when learning a new set of vocabulary words or reading a difficult text. The dictionary definition of a word can always be looked up to double-check intended meaning.

EXAMPLE

Read the following sentences and determine the meaning of the word *absorbed* based on context clues:

> Kamal was so *absorbed* by his video game that he didn't hear his grandmother calling him for dinner.

The dictionary definition of the word *absorbed* is "having one's attention fully engaged; greatly interested." In this sentence, the words "didn't hear" show that Kamal is not paying attention to anything other than what he's doing. The explanation that he's playing a video game tells us that he's most likely doing something he enjoys. The clues present in the sentence help the reader figure out that the word *absorbed* most likely means very interested. This word can also mean "liquid taken in or soaked up," but because Kamal is a person and not a liquid substance, the reader can determine that is not the correct meaning in this sentence.

SUBSTITUTION TO FIND MEANING

One way to find out if you have figured out the correct meaning of a new word is to **substitute** the meaning for the word. Using the example for *absorbed*, if the reader substituted in "very interested," the sentence would read:

> Kamal was so "very interested" by his video game that he didn't hear his grandmother calling him for dinner.

This is a way for the reader to confirm that they have used the context clues in the sentence correctly.

Multiple-Meaning Words

A multiple-meaning word has different **definitions** in the dictionary. Many words have multiple meanings, so the reader has to pay attention to how a word is used in a sentence to figure out which meaning is intended. A multiple-meaning word is spelled the same, no matter how it is used. So, to find the meaning of a multiple-meaning word, the reader needs to look at the information presented in the rest of the sentence. For example, look at the word *leaves* in the following two sentences:

- Michelle *leaves* the building at 5 o'clock every day.
- The *leaves* fell off the oak tree in September.

In the first sentence, *leaves* means exits. In the second sentence, *leaves* refers to parts of a tree. By looking at the rest of each sentence, the reader can understand which definition of the multiple-meaning word the author is referring to.

Example

Figure out the meaning of the multi-meaning word *part* from the context of the following sentence:

Anita wanted to have a *part* in figuring out when the school trip would take place.

Possible meanings of the word *part* include "piece," "quantity," and "role." The example sentence says that Anita wanted to have a *part* in figuring out when the school trip would take place." If the reader substitutes each meaning of the word *part* for the word itself, the reader can figure out that the correct meaning is "role." It is the only word that makes sense in this example sentence. Anita wanted to have a role in figuring out when the school trip would take place. "Role" is the correct meaning of *part* as used here.

Root Words, Prefixes, and Suffixes

The root, prefix, and suffix are parts of a word. The **root** is the main part of a word. It is what a **prefix** or **suffix** is attached to. A prefix goes on the front of a root word to make a new word. A suffix goes on the end of a root word to make a new word. Some words have both a prefix and a suffix. Many words have one or the other. The root, prefix, and suffix all have different meanings. By studying the parts of a word, the reader can figure out the meaning of a word.

Common Prefixes

Prefix	Meaning	Example
pre-	before	<u>pre</u>view (to view before)
im-	not	<u>im</u>possible (not possible)
non-	not	<u>non</u>paid (not paid)
dis-	not	<u>dis</u>agree (not agree)
in-	in, into, not	<u>in</u>justice (an action that is not just)

Common Suffixes

Suffix	Meaning	Example
-ness	state of being	dark<u>ness</u> (being dark)
-y	characterized by	cloud<u>y</u> (characterized by clouds)
-ful	full of	truth<u>ful</u> (full of truth)
-er	a person connected with	teach<u>er</u> (a person connected with teaching)
-able	can be done	like<u>able</u> (can be liked)

Example

Figure out the meaning of the word *unhappy* by using knowledge of words parts.

In the word *unhappy*, the root word *happy* means "pleased with." For instance, a student might be happy with his or her test score. The prefix *un-* means "not." The word *unhappy* means "not pleased." A student might be unhappy with a test score, too.

Example

Figure out the meaning of *harmful* from its word parts.

Harmful is made up of a root and a suffix. The root is *harm.* The word *harm* means "to hurt." The suffix is *-ful.* This suffix means "full of." A reader can figure out that the meaning of *harmful* is "full of hurt or harm."

Synonyms, Antonyms, Homophones, Homographs, and Idioms

Synonyms and Antonyms

Synonyms are words that have similar or the same meaning. For example, *happy* and *glad* mean the same thing, so they are synonyms. A word may have many synonyms. Other synonyms for *happy* are *content* and *pleased.*

Antonyms are words that have opposite meanings. For example, *big* is an antonym for *small.* A word may have many antonyms. Other antonyms for *little* are *large* and *huge.*

Here are some common words with possible synonyms and antonyms:

Word	Synonym	Antonym
Fast	Quick	Slow
Loud	Noisy	Soft
Pretty	Beautiful	Ugly
Rich	Wealthy	Poor
Sick	Unwell	Healthy
Start	Begin	End

Word	Synonym	Antonym
Tired	Sleepy	Energetic

Review Video: What are Synonyms and Antonyms?
Visit mometrix.com/academy and enter code: 105612

Example

Determine if there is a synonym or an antonym for the word *silly* in the following sentence:

> Danny was so silly that his teacher had to keep reminding him to be serious and stop fooling around.

To figure out if there is a synonym for *silly*, the reader needs to look at the context of the sentence. A synonym means the same as another word. Danny's teacher reminds him to "stop fooling around." The sentence also says that Danny "was so silly." The term *fooling around* means almost the same as *silly*. The reader can tell this from the context clues because context clues are hints. An antonym means the opposite of another word. The teacher tells Danny "to be serious." The reader can figure out that *serious* means the opposite of *silly*. The reader can tell that *serious* is an antonym of *silly* because the context gives clues about the meaning of *serious* and *silly*.

Homographs and Homophones

There are several types of words that sound alike but that have different meanings. **Homographs** are words that are spelled the same way, but have different meanings and that aren't always pronounced the same way. **Homophones** are words that sound alike, but are spelled differently and have different meanings.

Because some words have many meanings, the reader has to decide which meaning of the word is being used. To figure out which meaning is being used, the reader needs to look for context clues to find hints about the meaning of the word. For example, the word *spot* is a homograph. It can mean "a place" or "a stain or blot." In the sentence "After my lunch, I saw a spot on my shirt," the word *spot* means "a stain or blot." Context clues help the reader figure this out. The hints include "lunch" and "on my shirt."

Homographs

Homographs	
Quarter	
It's a quarter past noon.	I put a quarter in the vending machine.
Bat	
I love to watch bats fly through the sky.	I had practice today, but I forgot my bat.
Left	
Look both right and left before you cross the road.	The plane left for New York at three o'clock.

Homophones

Homophones	
Bare	Bear
The trees already look bare.	These parks are full of bears.
Blue	Blew
My favorite color is blue.	My coffee was too hot, so I blew on it.
Be	Bee
Be careful in the parking lot!	Look at the bee on that flower!

Idioms

Idioms create comparisons, and often look like similes or metaphors. An **idiom** is a phrase that has a meaning that is different from the literal meaning of its individual words. For example, "break a leg" is a common idiom that is used to wish someone luck or tell them to perform well. Literally, the phrase "break a leg" means to injure a person's leg, but the phrase takes on a different meaning when used as an idiom. Another example is "call it a day," which means to temporarily stop working on a task. The phrase does not mean to literally refer to something as "a day."

Chapter Quiz

1. A thesaurus can do all of the following, EXCEPT:

a. Give synonyms of words
b. Give word definitions
c. Help find the meaning of an unfamiliar word
d. Help authors vary their word choice when writing

2. Which of the following are words that sound alike, but are spelled differently and have different meanings?

a. Synonyms
b. Antonyms
c. Homophones
d. Homographs

3. What common suffix indicates state of being?

a. -ness
b. -y
c. -ful
d. -er

Chapter Quiz Answer Key

1. B: See section **Thesaurus**

2. C: See section **Homographs and Homophones**

3. A: See section **Common Suffixes**

Comprehension Skills

Generating Questions About Texts Before, During, and After Reading

Asking questions during the process of reading is one way for you to become a more **active reader**. Active readers do not just sit back and have the content handed to them. Instead, they get involved with the text and are part of the process of learning. Asking questions before you read, pausing to ask questions while you're reading, and asking questions after you read are all good ways to help you become a more active reader. There are three types of questioning that can use as you try to think of questions.

Questioning Yourself

These are questions you ask yourself to see how well you're paying attention, and how involved you are in the story. Some example questions are

- Which character is my favorite so far?
- What do I think is going to happen next?
- Is there a character I am similar to in this story? Do I like those similarities?
- What would I do if I was in this situation?

Questioning the Author

Although the chances are slim that you will ever get the chance to meet most of the authors of the texts you read, another way to get involved in the text is to imagine that you are asking questions of the author him or herself. Some example questions are

- What did the author want me to see here?
- Why did he write about this subject?
- Why did the author use this phrase?
- What did she want the character to learn from this?

Questioning the Text

The last type of question you can ask to improve your reading is called questioning the text. To ask these questions, imagine that you are asking the text itself questions about how it works and what it means. Some examples are:

- What does this word mean?
- What is this paragraph describing?
- Why is this term used here?
- How does this sentence connect to the other sentences in this paragraph?

Predicting What Will Happen in a Story

When you read a story, you should look for clues to make a prediction about what will happen. At the end of the story, you may even think about what will happen next to the main character, and use the clues in the story to make a prediction. You can also use personal experience to help make a prediction.

Suppose there is a story about a boy going swimming, and he swims too far out. Suppose the story says the boy can't get back to shore and starts to yell. Suppose the lifeguard comes and helps him. Suppose the story stops after the boy goes back in the water again. The reader might make the prediction that the boy won't swim as far out this time. This may not be true, but it is the most likely thing to happen.

Example

Describe what prediction can be made based on the following sentences:

> When Glen is sick, his mother keeps him home from school. He stays in bed all day and takes medicine. Glen woke up this morning with a sore throat. His head was hot, and he felt achy.

The story says that Glen's mother keeps him home when he is sick and that Glen spends the day in bed when he is sick. The story says that Glen woke up this morning with a sore throat. His head was hot, and he felt achy. The reader can figure out that Glen was sick. Because Glen's mother always keeps him home when he is sick, the reader can predict that Glen will be staying home from school and spending the day in bed.

You can also use text features find information to make predictions and verify conclusions determined about different texts. Using key words as clues, looking for bold print words, looking for sentences that include captions, and words that are written in italics are a few features that can be used to help understand and make predictions about a text.

Using Structure and Genre to Make Predictions

The structure and genre of a story can also help readers make predictions. Most stories follow the same structure. They have an exposition, rising action, a climax, falling action, and a resolution. Because most stories follow this structure, readers can predict that each of these parts will occur in the story. For example, rising action usually begins after the conflict of the story is introduced. This means that if characters have not faced any conflict, the reader can predict that something will go wrong for the characters. Likewise, stories in the same genre may contain similar events. For example, in a mystery, the characters work to solve a crime or explain a strange event. So, when reading a mystery, the reader can predict that the conflict will be a crime or event that the characters must learn more about.

Making Connections to Enhance Comprehension

Reading involves thinking. For good comprehension, readers make text-to-self, text-to-text, and text-to-world connections. Making connections helps readers understand text better and predict what might occur next based on what they already know, such as how characters in the story feel or what happened in another text. Readers can make connections before, during, and after reading. Venn diagrams and other graphic organizers can help readers visualize connections.

Text-to-Self

Reading while looking for connections with the reader's life and experiences makes literature more personally relevant and meaningful to readers. Sentences showing text-to-self connections may begin with these examples

- This reminds me of a time when...
- I understand how the character feels because...
- The setting makes me think of...
- I experienced this same thing when...

Text-to-Text

Reading while looking for connections to other texts helps the reader learn to identify the way authors use genre, setting, characters, plot elements, literary structure and devices, and themes to create meaning. Sentences showing text-to-text connections may begin with these examples

- The character in this story reminds me of the character in...
- These two stories are alike because...
- The conflict in this story is similar to the conflict in...
- The relationship between the friends in this story is different than the relationship in...

Text-to-World

Reading while looking for connections to the world helps the reader begin to see literature as a reflection of real life and notice patterns in history and current events. Sentences showing text-to-world connections may begin with these examples

- The event in this story sounds like the event in history when...
- The actions of this character sound like...
- This is like what happened in real life when...
- I heard about this on the news when...

Making Inferences

In a fictional work of literature, there are things that the author does not actually say, but hints at; the reader needs to connect the dots of these clues to draw a conclusion. This is called making an **inference**. An inference is a conclusion that the reader makes using clues in the text. An inference is different from making a guess, because inferences are based on evidence and guesses are random. When asked to infer something, the reader needs to use specific details from the text to show that their answer is supported.

For example, an author might mention that a character has a messy room and papers falling out of his binder. The reader can infer that the character is sloppy and disorganized even though the author does not **explicitly** state this fact.

Personal experience also helps a reader draw a conclusion. For example, suppose there is a story about two girls going to a movie. In the story, the girls are laughing at the end of the movie. This information helps a reader draw a conclusion, because they have likely laughed at a movie before. The conclusion is that the movie is funny. This may not be the reason the girls are laughing, but it seems likely. If the story said the girls had tears in their eyes at the end of the movie, a reader might conclude that the movie is sad.

Example

Describe what conclusion can be drawn based on the following sentences:

> Mr. Ted E. Bear was a hungry dog. He loved to eat his breakfast and his dinner. He would lap up his food in just minutes. One day his master forgot to feed him dinner because he had to meet someone. As the dog's master left, he noticed a sandwich on the table. When he got back, the sandwich was gone.

Conclusions are made based on the information in a story. A reader needs to find clues to form a conclusion about a story. This is a story about a hungry dog. The dog loves to eat. He is fed in the morning and the evening. His master forgets to feed him. His master goes out and leaves a sandwich on a table. When he comes back, the sandwich is gone. The conclusion a reader will draw is that the dog ate the sandwich. That is the most likely thing that happened to it. It may not be correct, but based on the information, it is the best conclusion.

Example

Describe what can be inferred from the following sentences:

> Sometimes after a big storm, the beaches are covered with dead fish, seaweed, broken shells, and pieces of wood. Most seaweed is brown or gold, but there are often pieces of white seaweed. If people visit the beaches, the white seaweed disappears very quickly. It makes a delicious pudding.

To make an inference a reader needs to look for clues in a text. The author does not tell an inference directly; the author hints at one. Here the text says that fish, seaweed, and shells are on the beach after a storm. It also says that some of the seaweed is white and adds that the white seaweed is used for pudding. Another clue is that the white seaweed disappears quickly if people visit the beaches. The inference that a reader can figure out is that the people take the seaweed. It disappears quickly because it can be used to make a delicious pudding.

Example

Read the following sentences and decide what evidence supports the conclusion that Tommy wasn't getting enough sleep:

> Tommy liked to sleep in his own bed. He had a hard time falling asleep in any other bed. Last week he visited his cousin. He stayed over for the weekend. At first, they had fun, but by the end of the weekend, Tommy was tired and grouchy. He wanted to go home.

The conclusion is that Tommy wasn't getting enough sleep. A reader needs to look for the evidence that the conclusion is true. A reader needs to find clues that support the conclusion. The story says that Tommy liked to sleep in his own bed and that he had trouble falling asleep in other beds. He visited his cousin for the weekend and ended up tired and grouchy. There are details in the story that support the conclusion that Tommy wasn't getting enough sleep. The detail that Tommy had a hard time falling asleep in another bed is one. The detail that Tommy was tired and grouchy at the end of the weekend is another.

Key Ideas and Supporting Details

Identifying **key ideas** helps the reader see what a text or story is mostly about. They are the **most important ideas** in a text, and everything else in the text builds around and supports them. Every piece of writing has key ideas. The **supporting details** in a story, such as the characters, events, and settings, will work together to reveal the key ideas. The details are not key ideas, themselves. They make the key ideas clear and show the reader the author's purpose for writing the text.

Synthesizing a Text with Existing Knowledge

Synthesizing is similar to summarizing but it takes it one step further. Synthesizing involves taking the main points of a text and comparing it with existing knowledge to create a new idea, perspective, or way of thinking.

EXAMPLE

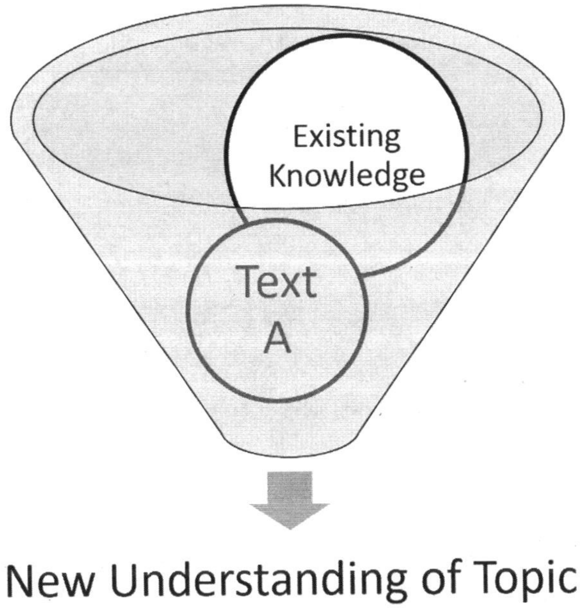

Another term for knowledge that you already have is **schema**. The plural form of this word is **schemata**. Schemata contain all the ideas you have about something. Synthesizing is all about how schemata change over time with the introduction of new information.

Using self-questioning strategies can help readers synthesize texts with their schemata to increase or change their understanding of topics. These questions include

- What do I already know about this topic?
- Is any of this new information?
- Has my perspective changed now that I've read this?
- What do I understand now that I didn't before?
- What are the main ideas of this text?
- How do the parts of the text fit together to create meaning?
- Are there any text-to-text, text-to-self, or text-to-world connections here?

SYNTHESIZING TEXTS WITHOUT EXISTING KNOWLEDGE

If the reader is completely unfamiliar with the topic, they will have no background knowledge. In this case, instead of using existing knowledge, synthesizing may instead be done by combining the ideas provided in two or three different texts. The reader must make connections between the texts, determine how the ideas fit together, and gather evidence to support the new perspective.

CHAPTER QUIZ

1. There are three types of questioning that you can use for active reading. What are these three types of questions?

a. Questioning the composition, grammar, and style of the writing
b. Questioning history, current events, and the future
c. Questioning your personal context, surrounding culture, and the world
d. Questioning yourself, the author, and the text

2. Which of the following helps the reader learn to identify ways authors use genre, setting, characters, plot elements, literary structure and devices, and themes to create meaning?

a. Reading while looking for connections to the reader's life
b. Reading while looking for connections to other texts
c. Reading while looking for connections to the world
d. Reading while looking for connections to history

3. Which of the following is a conclusion that the reader makes using clues in the text?

a. Thesis
b. Prediction
c. Inference
d. Guess

4. What term refers to knowledge that you already have?

a. Cognition
b. Glossary
c. Schema
d. Explicit information

Chapter Quiz Answer Key

1. D: See section **Generating Questions About Texts Before, During, and After Reading**

2. B: See section **Making Connections to Enhance Comprehension**

3. C: See section **Making Inferences**

4. C: See section **Synthesizing a Text with Existing Knowledge**

Response Skills

Text Evidence

The term **text evidence** refers to information found in a text that supports a reader's claim about the text. A reader can draw conclusions or inferences based upon information found in a text. Often, the author will deliberately include information that supports the main point of the text to help the reader make conclusions and inferences that align with the author's purpose for writing the text.

Drawing Conclusions Based on Text Evidence

Readers often need to use prior experience and background information to draw an accurate conclusion about the passage they are reading. Sometimes interpreting the information in a sentence can be difficult, especially if the reader is unfamiliar with some of the words used in a sentence. Looking at the words that the reader does understand in the sentence can help. By taking a pen or pencil and underlining important information in a sentence, the reader can better understand what the author is trying to say and draw a clearer conclusion from that.

EXAMPLE

Draw a conclusion based on the following quote from *Flora & Ulysses: The Illuminated Adventures* by Kate DiCamillo

> Take this squirrel, for instance. Ulysses. Do I believe he can type poetry? Sure, I do believe it. There is much more beauty in the world if I believe such a thing is possible.

This quote is from the character Dr. Meescham, who is speaking to Flora about her squirrel, Ulysses. Saying a squirrel can type seems silly, but the doctor says he does believe it's true. The phrase "there is much more beauty... if I believe" helps the reader draw the conclusion that Dr. Meescham encourages imagination, and that seeing the world as beautiful is important. The things characters say often show something important about them. Be sure to read dialogue carefully to see what conclusions the author might be wanting you to make.

EXAMPLE

Read the following quote from *Shiloh* by Phyliss Reynolds Naylor and draw a conclusion based upon the information presented.

> Last of all, I take the lard bread from my pocket and feed it to Shiloh in little pieces, letting him lick my fingers after every bite. I wrap my arms around him, pat him, run my hands over his ears, even kiss his nose. I tell him about a million times I love him as much as I love my ma.

The reader can conclude that the narrator adores his dog Shiloh. The words "wrap my arms around him," "kiss his nose," and "tell him about a million times I love him" lead the reader to this conclusion. The reader can also assume that Shiloh loves the narrator as well because he allows all of the touches that he is receiving. Readers know from experience that animals do not often allow touch from people they do not have affection for.

When interpreting a sentence, always look for key phrases that can be used to draw conclusions about characters and their relationships. Authors carefully craft descriptions of each character to form a picture in the reader's mind about what the character is like.

PARAPHRASING AND SUMMARIZING

Paraphrasing and summarizing are two ways readers can work to understand what they read. Both involve reading a text and recalling the main points in an accurate way, but they differ in several ways.

How to Paraphrase	How to Summarize
State the message in the text in the reader's own words, while keeping the original meaning of the text Take all of the original ideas and word them in a way that the reader can better understand Put what the reader has read into their own words, rephrasing what the author has written	State main points of the text clearly and to-the-point. Take information and state it simply, in a much shorter form. Put information in a short form that keeps the main points of the whole text. Do not include many details, just the main idea of the text

Paraphrasing is often done for individual ideas, while summarizing is done for an entire block of text or ideas. Often times, a summary can be done in just one sentence, boiling down the author's words into just main idea.

Paraphrasing the Main Point of a Sentence

Paraphrase the main point of the following two sentences:

> Emmanuel went swimming in the lake by his house, where the water reached a depth of twenty feet in the middle. He did not venture out more than six feet into the water, however.

When paraphrasing a couple sentences or an entire paragraph, always include the main point of the text being reviewed, this is what the reader needs to know about the text. In the example, the reader needs to know that Emmanuel went swimming in the lake, but not more than six feet out. A paraphrase of the text may include: Emmanuel went swimming six feet out in the lake by his house. That is the main point that the audience needs to know.

Recall that a paraphrase is stating the author's ideas in the reader's own words. A summary typically involves including the main points of a longer text, such as a novel or full story.

Example

Read the following paragraph and then give a one sentence summary statement:

> When choosing a pet, people need to think about what type of home they can offer the animal. For example, a small apartment might not be a good fit for a large dog, but could be a comfortable home for a kitten. A house that has a big yard would be great for a puppy, but a rabbit does not need a large yard.

In order to summarize, one has to identify the main idea and any supporting ideas in the author's work. The summary is an overview of the author's paragraph and will tell what it is about without getting into any of the details. The summary needs to be broad enough to cover all of the information in the author's paragraph. Here is a possible summary statement for the above paragraph:

> People need to consider a number of factors when choosing a pet.

Chapter Quiz

1. If a reader takes an author's original idea and then restates it, putting the idea into their own words, this is an example of:

a. Outlining text
b. Paraphrasing text
c. Summarizing text
d. Abstracting text

2. Which of the following is NOT true of summarizing?

a. A summary can be just one sentence that boils down the author's words into the main idea.
b. Summarizing helps readers work to understand what they have read.
c. A summary typically involves restating the main points of a text in a simpler, shorter fashion.
d. A summary should be subjective and include brief personal opinions on the subject.

Chapter Quiz Answer Key

1. B: See section **Paraphrasing and Summarizing**

2. D: See section **Paraphrasing and Summarizing**

Literary Elements

Theme

The **theme** of a story, essay, or poem is the lesson that it teaches, or the message the author wants to get across. The theme is linked to the characters, the setting, and the events in a story. Some themes are fairly common. These themes are called **universal themes** and they suggest things about life, society, and human nature.

The theme of a story is not the same as the topic of a story. The topic is what the story is about, but the theme is what a reader is meant to learn. Themes are very rarely stated in the text. Instead, the reader has to **infer** the theme by reading closely and thinking carefully about what the author is saying.

Themes are an important part of literature because they serve the purpose of teaching the reader or listener a truth about life. The theme is developed by how a character or characters respond to their situations and challenges.

Example

Read the following and consider the theme of the excerpt.

> Jeanie arrived at the bake sale early. She bought the biggest cake at the sale. Sally had to work late. When she finally got to the sale, no cakes were left. She got only two cookies. She was lucky to get anything.

The saying "the early bird gets the worm" is one way to explain the theme of the story. In the story we read that Jeanie arrived early at the bake sale and got the biggest cake. But when Sally arrived, all that was left were two cookies. The point of the story is that the early bird gets the worm—the worm in this case is a large cake. In this story, the topic is a bake sale, but the theme is not "bake sale" because the words "bake sale" do not teach the reader anything.

Characters

Character Relationships

A relationship is the way one character acts with another character in a story. The characters are often called **major characters** if they have a main part in the story and **minor characters** if they have a smaller part. There are many different kinds of relationships. For example, two children in a story may be friends, but they could be angry with each other, competing with each other, or helping each other. An author may tell the reader what kind of relationship the characters have. An author might give hints about a relationship. For example, the author may show one child making fun of the other child, which would suggest that the two children do not have a friendly relationship. The author might show one child teaching the other child how to read, which would suggest that the two children have a friendly relationship.

Example

Read the following sentences and describe the relationship Jill and Anna have:

> Jill came over to Anna and asked if she wanted an apple. "Sure, I'd love one. Thanks," Anna answered. Anna took a bite of the apple and started to chew it. Her chewing was so loud that they both started to laugh.

The author does not tell what the relationship between Jill and Anna is. The reader must figure it out from their actions. These actions are the clues the author gives. Jill asks Anna if she wants an apple. Anna says yes and starts to eat it. Her chewing is very loud. Both Jill and Anna start to laugh. They seem to like each other. Jill seems generous to Anna because she gives Anna an apple. They laugh together, and friends often laugh together. The reader can use personal experience to decide that it seems as though Jill and Anna are friends.

Characters' Feelings

An author can show how a character feels in many ways. For example, the character may laugh a lot, which shows that the character is happy. The character could cry, which shows that the character is sad. There are other ways an author shows a character's feelings. A character may say something that shows he or she is sad. For example, a character may say that she misses her old school. This statement would show that the character is sad. A character may say something about enjoying her new school. This statement would show that the character is happy. An author knows that a character's feelings are important in a story. Sometimes the author says how a character is feeling; other times the author gives hints or clues about what a character feels.

Example

Read the following sentences and describe how Lorna feels:

> Lorna walked forward very slowly. The strange scratching noise was growing louder. She thought about calling out for help, but she knew no one would hear her. She decided to keep going anyway.

The author does not tell the reader directly how Lorna feels, but there are many clues about how Lorna feels from her actions. The sentences say that Lorna walks forward slowly and that there is a strange scratching noise. The sentence also says that she thinks about calling for help. These clues all suggest that Lorna is frightened. She doesn't know what is making the scratching noise. She wants to call for help, but she cannot. She is scared. The sentences also suggest another feeling. Lorna doesn't run away. She decides to keep going. This is another clue. It shows that Lorna is also feeling brave.

Plot

The term **plot** refers to the series of events that take place in a story. The events in a story may take place in one location or many, in a short amount of time or over many years. A story always has to start somewhere, and the first event in a story signals the beginning of the plot. Stories may vary in length from half a page to novel-length, but they all follow a progression of events that the author winds together to form the plot. The characters and events in the story determine what the plot will be. Readers may find a **plot line** useful as they try to put the events in the text in order and determine the relationships between events.

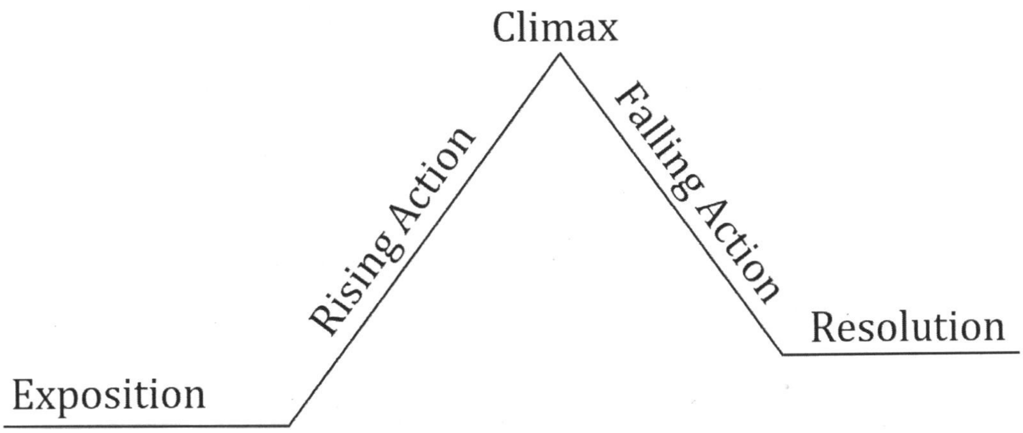

Review Video: Plot Line
Visit mometrix.com/academy and enter code: 944011

Every plot will begin with **exposition**, which introduces the characters and the setting of the story. The plot will continue to develop as new ideas and events centered on the main conflict in the story are revealed, which is called the **rising action**. The action in the story will rise until a **climax** is reached within the conflict. The climax can also be referred to as the turning point in the story, since the climax is where each character makes an important decision. After the climax, the action starts to wind down during the **falling action**. At this point, the characters begin to follow the paths they chose in during climax. The events of the story reach **resolution** in some way by the end of the story. Some conflicts are left open-ended, so that the reader is left to decide what really happened at the end of the story. Keep in mind that not all resolutions are happy or peaceful.

EXAMPLE

Read the following plot and determine what the missing event is in the plot sequence:

> Sarita went to the store to buy eggs for her mother. She bought the eggs and got back on her bicycle to bring the eggs home. Her mother was angry that the eggs were all broken.

The reader has to guess based on the plot sequence what happened between events. The reader knows that Sarita got on her bicycle to go home. The reader also knows that the eggs were broken when she arrived at the house. Based on the context, the reader can assume that Sarita fell off her bicycle or dropped the eggs on the way home, causing them to all be broken when she arrived. The reader can assume that Sarita would have noticed if the eggs were already broken in the store. Plot often follows a logical sequence of events, but sometimes it is difficult to decide what actually happened between two events. In the example, the reader can logically assume that the eggs were broken on the way home.

CONFLICT

Conflict creates the basis for the plot of a story. A conflict may be between characters, a character and their own mind, or an outside influence. The main point of a conflict is that there is a problem that needs to be resolved. The problem may be a disagreement or an obstacle that has arisen and needs to be overcome.

An important part of analyzing the plot of a passage is identifying the **main conflict**. There will likely be many smaller conflicts in the story, but there will be one main problem that influences the characters and events. To identify the main conflict, first look at who the main character is. Now ask yourself what they want. They may want to something to happen or not happen, another character to do or not do something, or to confront or avoid a problem, among other things. Once you know what they want, now ask yourself what is standing in the character's way. It may be a person, an event, or something less tangible like the passing of time. Combining what the main character wants and why they do not currently have leaves the reader with a summary of the main conflict.

Example

Read the following sentence and explain the main conflict between the two characters:

> Joe stared angrily at Jamie's retreating back as Jamie raced away down the field with Joe's soccer ball.

The main conflict in the sentence is that Jamie has Joe's soccer ball. There may be additional conflicts between the two characters, but none are evident from the evidence shown in the sentence. In any story, a conflict may be minor and only affect part of the story, or be the main focus, taking an entire story to solve a conflict between characters. In the context of the sentence, it is not clear whether or not the entire story will revolve around Jamie taking Joe's soccer ball.

Resolution

The term **resolution** usually indicates the result of a conflict in a story. Conflict between characters, within a character, or against an external element is necessary in order to have a plot for a story. Without conflict, no events would occur to form the story. A conflict will come to a climax, and then conclude in some way. The resolution of a problem may be open-ended, end tragically, or end in a way that is good for everyone involved. The problem resolution typically occurs near the end of a story, after the climax has happened. A problem may be resolved by the characters involved within the conflict or by an external event; an upcoming resolution may be foreshadowed in the text, or may be completely unexpected by the reader. If the resolution is completely unexpected, it is considered to be a **twist** in the story.

Effect of Plot on a Story's Characters

The plot of a story unfolds as each event follows another, shaping the characters as they react to the various events that occur. Some characters are able to resolve their problems by the end of the story, while some characters fail to overcome their predicaments. As characters respond to the events around them, they reveal more and more about their personalities. Some grow and some do not. The reader can use the events of the plot to interpret the meaning of the story and understand its characters.

Example

Read the excerpt and explain how finding the chest affects Marta.

> The map said this was the spot. Marta held her breath. Her fists were clenched into two tight balls. She lifted the shovel and scooped more sand out of the hole. There it was; she had found the chest with the diamonds. She opened the top. She would never need to work again. She smiled. It was really happening.

The event affects Marta by making her happy. The reader gets several clues that she is anxiously waiting ("Marta held her breath" and "her fists were clenched"), and that she is happy with what she found ("She smiled"). Events can cause characters to have all kinds of feelings. Here, something wonderful happened. However, events in stories are not always quite so happy. For instance, if a robber had suddenly seen Marta and the chest, he might have stolen the chest. That event would have had a very different effect on her. Readers need to pay attention to how characters are reacting to events, whether they are simply hinted at or stated in the story. In this way a reader will learn what characters are like.

SETTING

The setting is where a story **takes place**. The setting of a story may stay the same for the entire story, or change as events in the story unfold. For example, an entire story may take place in one room, or on the other end, a story could cross continents as the reader follows the characters along on a trail of events. Every story has to take place somewhere. The setting of story is described by the author in terms of what it looks like, how the character feels, and anything that is happening at that location at the time. For example, a character may be caught on a doorstep on a cold, rainy day. The character may feel frustrated as he shivers in the doorway, waiting for the heavy rain to let up a bit.

EXAMPLE

When listing ways that a story set in the city has a different backdrop from a story set in the countryside, answers will vary based on current knowledge of common characteristics for each setting. A story set in a city may be different from a story set in the countryside based on the following factors:

- Number of passersby: many people on a sidewalk vs. no other people around
- Background noise: car horns vs. bird calls
- Types of surroundings: tall buildings vs. fields of corn
- Types of transportation: subways and taxis vs. horses and farm trucks
- Daily activities being carried out: sitting at a desk in a skyscraper vs. plowing fields for planting
- Type of attire: a business suit vs. dirty jeans and boots

SHAPING A CHARACTER WITH SETTING OR PLOT

The setting of a story shapes character because it helps to define the situation that a character finds herself in. A character is limited to the setting of a story. For example, if a story takes place in a cold environment filled with snow and ice, this is certain to impact what actions a character can and will take. Frequently, the setting changes the way characters behave based on time. For example, the character of a woman who is a single mother in 1920 would be seen and behave very differently than a single mother in 2020.

EXAMPLE

Read the excerpt and determine how the setting influences the character in this excerpt.

> She had swum too far out. The waves were higher than she thought. She was struggling hard to get to shore. She wondered if she would make it. She thought of her childhood. Had she been right to run away from home, she wondered? Just then, a lifeguard grabbed her and helped her to shore.

The setting of the ocean and the high waves creates a conflict in the character. She is worried. She thinks about her childhood and her parents. She doesn't know if she will make it to shore. This is how the setting affects the character in this excerpt. Without the high waves and the struggle, she would not become so worried and start to think about her past. She probably would not have questioned herself. This is an example of how a setting influences a character. If the waves had not been high, there probably would not have been a struggle or any self-searching of the swimmer's past.

CHAPTER QUIZ

1. Which of the following is the lesson that a story teaches, or the message the author wants to get across?

a. Theme
b. Setting
c. Topic
d. Plot

2. Every plot will begin with __________, which introduces the characters and the setting of the story.

a. Conflict
b. Rising action
c. Foreshadowing
d. Exposition

CHAPTER QUIZ ANSWER KEY

1. A: See section **Theme**

2. D: See section **Plot**

Literary Genres

CHILDREN'S LITERATURE

There are types of texts that are specifically meant to be read by children or younger audiences. Children's literature contains many different **genres**, which are categories that texts can be divided into. Some types of children's literature are

- **Folktales** -Songs, stories, myths, or proverbs belonging to a group of people. Often passed down from generation to generation by word of mouth.
- **Fairy tales** are stories that include fictional creatures or characters with fantastical traits and abilities. Fairy tales often end happily and depict the victory of good over evil. The plots and characters in fairy tales are often far-fetched and whimsical.
- **Fables** –Story told (often by a narrator) full of supernatural features like speaking animals. The tale demonstrates a useful truth at the end.
- **Legends** -A story featuring a national or folk hero. Often has a basis in actual fact, but also contains imaginative material.
- **Myth** -A legend or traditional narrative, often based on a historical event. The story reveals something about human behavior or the natural world, and often involves actions of gods.
- **Tall Tales** -A story full of outlandish exaggerations, often humorous and containing heroes who perform impossible acts easily.

POETRY

POET VERSUS SPEAKER

The author of a poem is called a **poet**. Many poems are written in first person, which means the **stanzas** (groups of lines) include words like "I" and "me." However, the poet is not always the

speaker of the poem. In a novel, the author can create characters with different points of view. The characters can argue or have different roles to play in telling the story. Similarly, a poet may write a poem from a different point of view or even include more than one voice. The speaker is the voice of the poem, and is not always the same person as the poet him or herself. The reader or listener should know that the person telling the story is a character, and not always a real person.

For example, this excerpt from a poem by Dr. Seuss reads:

> When you think things are bad,
> when you feel sour and blue,
> when you start to get mad...
> you should do what I do!
> Just tell yourself, Duckie,
> you're really quite lucky!
> Some people are much more...
> oh, ever so much more...
> oh, muchly much-much more
> unlucky than you!

Even though one line has the word "I" in it, the poem is not from the perspective of Dr. Seuss. He is the author of the poem, but not the speaker. The person saying "I" is a character, just like in a story.

RHYME IN POETRY

Poets use rhymes to help readers understand poems. Words **rhyme** when they sound similar to each other, especially when the similar sound is at the end of the words, like *cat* and *hat*, or *roar* and *soar*. Rhyming words usually have endings that are spelled the same way, but sometimes they are spelled differently, like *wait* and *hate* or *bear* and *snare*.

Famous poet Shel Silverstein uses rhyme in many of his poems. For example, in his poem "Listen to the Mustn'ts", the last word of the first- and second-lines rhyme with each other, and the last word of the third- and fourth-line rhyme with each other.

> Listen to Mustn'ts, child, listen to the Don'ts.
> Listen to the Shouldn'ts, the Impossibles, the Won'ts.
> Listen to the Never Haves, then listen close to me.
> Anything can happen, child, Anything can be.

The pattern of the rhymes in this poem forms a **rhyme scheme**. Sometimes poets use a rhyme scheme that makes every other line of the poem rhyme instead.

SOUND DEVICES IN POETRY

Sound devices allow authors to add more meaning to their poems by tapping into the spoken part of language. Authors may use many sound devices to create meaning and help readers understand them better, including:

ALLITERATION

- Appeals to the reader's sense of hearing by using words that begin with the same consonant sound in a sentence or in a line of poetry.
- For example, the popular tongue-twister "She sells sea shells by the seashore" uses words that only begin with the sound that the letter 's' makes.

- An author could choose to make their alliteration less noticeable by writing "The green crocodile moved gradually towards me, his greedy smile giving me goosebumps." In this sentence, the sound that the letter "g" makes is repeated throughout the sentence, making it alliterative even though the words beginning with 'g' are not right next to each other.

> **Review Video: Alliteration in Everyday Expressions**
> Visit mometrix.com/academy and enter code: 462837

DRAMA

Dramas are texts that are written to be performed by people reading the lines or acting the stories out. They can also be presented as monologues (one character speaks), dialogues (two character speak to each other), or pantomimes (body movements are used instead of spoken words). Dramatic texts are called plays or **scripts**, and they are written differently than other texts.

TEXT STRUCTURE IN DRAMA

Plays are divided into **acts** (large units) and **scenes** (small sections inside acts) instead of chapters. There are also **stage directions**, which are instructions from the playwright about where items go, where actors should move, and what the characters should be doing during the scene. Stage directions are usually in italics to set them apart from other parts of the play. When it is time for a character in a play to speak, there will be **character tag** on the left side of the page which shows the name of the character (all letters of the name are capitalized) followed by a colon.

Here is an example of how a page from a play might look:

Title of Play

Act Number

Scene Number

The setting of the scene is being described here. The reader is being introduced to the characters and the things happening around them. Characters will enter speak to one another during the scene.

CHARACTER 1:

I am speaking. These are words I say. *(stage directions)* I am still speaking.

CHARACTER 2 *enters and does something.*

CHARACTER 2:

Now I am speaking. This is my dialogue.

DIALOGUE AND STAGE DIRECTIONS

Dialogue refers to what the characters say in a play when they are talking to each other, talking to themselves, or even talking to the audience. The type of speech, word choice, and accent a character uses is specific to the role he is playing. For example, a person cast to play a cowboy would have certain words in his vocabulary that a character from a big city in the North would not have.

A playwright also uses stage directions to make the play flow smoothly. Character interaction helps the viewer to understand the mood of the scene. If two characters are confrontational, the viewer is aware that there is some type of conflict occurring. Stage directions create order when all the characters are on stage together.

Informational Text

Controlling Idea

The controlling idea, also called the main idea or thesis, of a passage is usually located in the first paragraph or two of text. Having the controlling idea near the beginning of the passage allows the author to grab the reader's attention and let them know what the rest of the passage will discuss.

To find the controlling idea in a passage, there are questions the reader can ask while reading: What is this passage about? What does the author want the reader to know about the topic? The supporting details will provide evidence that the controlling idea is correct and are found in the body of a passage. The supporting details often provide examples of the controlling idea.

Supporting Details

Supporting details provide evidence and backing for the controlling idea. All texts contain details, but they are only classified as supporting details when they serve to reinforce some larger point. Supporting details are most commonly found in informative and persuasive texts. In some cases, they will be clearly indicated with words like for example or for instance, or they will be enumerated with words like first, second, and last. However, these special words are not a requirement. As a reader, it is important to consider whether the author's supporting details really back up his or her main point. Supporting details can be factual and correct but still not relevant to the author's point. Sometimes, supporting details can seem important but they might not support the main idea in the story well because they are based on opinion that cannot be proven.

Example

Read the following two sentences. State which sentence is a main idea and which sentence is a supporting detail. Explain the difference between the two sentences:

> She went fishing with her cousin Vinny.
>
> Jayden visited her relatives in Louisiana over the summer.

The first sentence is a supporting detail, and the second sentence is the main idea. A main idea gives the overall concept, or point, of the story. A supporting detail adds more information to the point of the story. The reader already knows that the name of the character needs to be introduced before using the pronoun she. Therefore, it makes sense that Jayden visiting her relatives in Louisiana over the summer must come before the supporting detail about her going fishing with her cousin Vinny. Once the reader knows the overall point of the text, supporting details help to explain what else happens in the story. The reader knows from the main point that the character Jayden is visiting her relatives in Louisiana, which is where she went fishing.

Example

Read the following main idea of a story and write a supporting detail for it:

> Madison's favorite thing to talk about was strawberries.

A good supporting detail would need to include information that supports or explains more about the main idea. A supporting detail might read: "She also loved to eat them," or "She also grew strawberries in her backyard." Supporting details provide additional information about the main idea that has not already been presented to the reader. A supporting detail further develops the topic of the story and provides an explanation of a part of the main idea.

In the example supporting details above, note that the topic is still focused on the subject of strawberries and action that the character takes in relation to that particular subject. A main idea will often appear in the first one to two paragraphs of a story. Supporting details appear later in a paragraph or in other paragraphs within the story.

Structural Features of Informational Text

Texts which intend to inform the reader about a topic are often accompanied by visual aids or graphics. Some common examples are listed below.

- **Insets and sidebars** show additional information related to the text in boxes or on the sides of the page. Insets can contain pictures or text, and sometimes have different colored backgrounds or font types to make them stand out from the text.
- **Timelines** are a visual aid which show how events from the text happened over time, and usually contain dates, locations, or other related information.
- **Tables** are visual aids that organize information in a way that shows the relationship between the information. Tables are made using rows and columns, and the pieces in the rows and columns are called cells. Usually, the first row or column will contain a title or heading that categorizes or defines the other cells in that row or column.
- **Bullet points** list items separately, making facts and ideas easier to see and understand.
- **Numbers** can also be used to list separate items. Usually, numbers are used to show that the items are part of a sequence. For example, in a list of instructions, each instruction may be numbered to show the reader the order in which each instruction should be completed.
- **Italics** are a formatting technique that makes text appear slanted. Italics can be used to emphasize text because they cause the text to look different and lead the reader to notice it more easily. Italics are also often used in fiction to show that text is part of a character's thoughts. They are also commonly used to show that a word or section of text is written in a foreign language.
- **Boldface** is a way to format text to make it stand out. Boldface, or bold, text can be used to emphasize a word, phrase, or idea. Boldface can also be used to let the reader know that they can find more information about a term in a glossary, sidebar, or other feature of the text.

Organizational Patterns

Authors want to have an effective text that the reader can understand. If ideas do not follow a logical order, the reader will become confused and not know what the author is trying to say. When writing, there are a variety of ways that an author can choose to organize a written work. It is important to choose the pattern that best presents the information, as not all patterns will work for every piece of writing. An author may organize ideas according to a timeline, cause and effect, or description of an event or setting.

Order of Importance

The author puts the information in the text in order of what is most important. Order of importance can be either increasing or decreasing, depending on how the writer wants to structure the work.

Chronological Order

The author organizes the progression of events based upon when they occurred and what was included in each step of the story. By organizing the text in this way the author presents all necessary information about the six questions readers can ask to help themselves understand the text: who, what, when, where, why, and how.

PROBLEM AND SOLUTION

The author presents some information as a problem and then discusses a solution or attempted solution to that problem. In problem and solution, there is generally one main problem, but that one problem may have several possible solutions.

For example, suppose Billy wants a new video game but does not have the money. There are several possible solutions to this. He might try asking his mom to buy it for him. If that does not work, he could offer to do small jobs to earn enough money to buy it. A third possibility might be to wait until his birthday and ask for it then.

CAUSE AND EFFECT

The author will write about relationship between two events that occur, where the second event occurs as a result of the first.

For example, a text may discuss a school policy stating that when a student is late to school too many times, they receive a detention. Later in the text, we might see a student repeatedly arriving late to school, after which he is given a detention. In this example, the **cause** is the student being late to school, and the **effect** is the student receiving a detention.

COMPARE AND CONTRAST

The author will show similarities and differences between items or events.

For example, the author may write about cats and dogs. They might start by giving a brief description of the two. Then they will want to point out all of the similarities, such as; they both have tails, and both are kept as pets. Next, they will explain the differences, such as; dogs are canines, while cats are felines. They will try to provide as much detail as possible about both the similarities and the differences.

IDENTIFYING ORGANIZATIONAL PATTERNS

EXAMPLE

Read the following paragraph from a story. Describe how the author organizes information in the paragraph:

> First, John stopped at the grocery store to pick up some bread. Next, he went home and checked the mail. Finally, John sat down on the couch and opened up a book to where he had stopped reading.

The author uses chronological order to present information to the reader. The points in the story follow the order in which they occurred in time. The reader can look for words that give a clue as to progression of time, such as first, next, and finally. The paragraph does not use cause and effect, because one event does not lead to the occurrence of another. Each event is separate based upon when it occurred during the day. A progression of events can be placed on a timeline, to provide a visual image of when each event occurred. This is a helpful way to organize information in a lengthy story. The information in the paragraph is not overly descriptive, nor does it show where each event occurred in relation to another.

EXAMPLE

Read the following paragraph from a news story and describe how the author organizes information in the story:

> The parade in honor of the town's 200th anniversary began at the corner of 57th Street at 9:00 a.m. on Saturday morning. Members of the fire department led the parade, dressed in their bright red hats and heavy yellow coats. At 9:15 a.m., members of the high school band gave a performance.

The news story uses chronological order organize ideas. The reader is given information about what type of event occurred, when the event occurred, what the event was about, and who was included.

EXAMPLE

Identify organizational pattern that is used in the following sentence from *Morte d'Arthur* by Sir Thomas Malory:

> The king had given his promise, so he was obliged to agree.

The text structure of cause and effect is used in this sentence. The cause in the sentence is that the king gave his promise, and the effect is that he had to agree.

ARGUMENTATIVE TEXTS

IDENTIFYING THE CLAIM

In a persuasive or argumentative text, the author is writing in order to make and support a claim. A claim is similar to the key idea of an informational text. However, a claim can be argued, which means that some readers may not agree with it. The author of the text will need to use the body of the text to support the claim and show readers why they should agree with it. To identify the claim of a text, first identify the topic. Then, read the introduction text to see what the author writes about the topic.

The claim should be clearly stated in the introduction. However, if the claim is still not clear, read the body to see what kind of evidence the author uses to support the claim. The way that the author gives and applies evidence may also show what the claim of the text is.

CALL TO ACTION

Another strategy is to look for a call to action in the text. A call to action is a statement that instructs the reader to do something after reading the text. Often, the call to action will tell the reader to do something that shows that he or she agrees with the author's claim. For example, if an author's claim is that reading is better than watching a movie, the author may include a call to action that says "Turn off the TV and dig in to a new book today!" By including this statement, the author is telling the readers to show their agreement by choosing to read rather than watch a movie.

FACT AND OPINION

When deciding whether information is fact or opinion, a reader needs to look at whether or not the information is well-accepted by experts, in addition to being backed-up by outside sources. A fact is something that is true, regardless of what the author thinks, on the contrary, an opinion is what the author thinks, without regard to evidence to back-up that claim.

For example, in a paper about caves, a fact may read: Extensive cave systems run through the soft limestone of Central Texas. An opinion may read: Caving, also called spelunking, is an enjoyable recreational activity. It is a fact that caves run throughout Central Texas, but it is the author's opinion that spelunking is an enjoyable recreational activity.

Identifying the Intended Audience

Authors of persuasive and argumentative texts want to convince others to agree with a claim or take a certain action. Because of this, they will often write to a specific audience. Often, the target audience will include people who disagree with the author's claim. The author's desire is to give these people information that will lead them to change their minds or actions.

Strategies for Identifying the Intended Audience

One way to identify the intended audience of a persuasive or argumentative text is to first identify the author's claim. Then, consider who would disagree with the author's claim. This group of people is likely the group that the author wants to persuade.

Another way to identify the audience is to look for clues in the text. Sometimes, authors will clearly state which people are included in the intended audience. For example, imagine that an author includes the statement, "Teachers should reward their students every time they make a good grade on a test." This shows that the text is written for teachers who do not already reward their students for good test grades. Similarly, a call to action may show who the target audience is by instructing the members of the audience to take a certain action.

Chapter Quiz

1. What type of children's literature can be described as songs, stories, myths, or proverbs belonging to a group of people, that are often passed down from generation to generation by word of mouth?

a. Folktales
b. Fables
c. Legends
d. Tall tales

2. In poetry, which of the following appeals to the reader's sense of hearing by using words that begin with the same consonant sound in a sentence or in a line of poetry?

a. Assonance
b. Rhyme
c. Line breaks
d. Alliteration

3. In dramatic texts (plays or scripts), which of the following are usually in italics to set them apart from other parts of the play?

a. Dialogues
b. Acts and scenes
c. Stage directions
d. Character tags

4. What structural feature is used to list items separately, making facts and ideas easier to see and understand?

a. Boldface
b. Bullet points
c. Sidebars
d. Headings

5. If an author writes about cats and dogs, showing their similarities and differences, this would be an example of what type of organizational pattern?

a. Cause and effect
b. Problem and solution
c. Proposition and support
d. Compare and contrast

CHAPTER QUIZ ANSWER KEY

1. A: See section **Children's Literature**

2. D: See section **Alliteration**

3. C: See section **Text Structure in Drama**

4. B: See section **Structural Features of Informational Text**

5. D: See section **Compare and Contrast**

Author's Purpose and Craft

AUTHOR'S PURPOSE

An author may write a text for many different purposes. Four of the most common purposes are to inform, to persuade or influence, to express, or to entertain readers.

	Definition	Example
Informational Texts	Inform the reader on a topic that they previously knew nothing about, such as many non-fiction texts.	An informative paper on kangaroos would detail where kangaroos live, what they look like, what they eat, and other habits.
Persuasive Texts	Influence the reader to think a certain way about a topic, calling them to action or pointing them toward resources that would help them to learn more about the topic.	An author may try to persuade the reader that waterparks are the best place to go in the summer when it is hot outside. The author would present information about waterparks and explain *why* they are good places to visit.
Expressive Texts	Express the author or speaker's opinion or emotions about a topic. Lots of descriptive words are used to clearly show the reader how the author or speaker feels.	The author may think that a new playground in town is a good idea, and write an essay about why a playground would be great for the community.
Entertaining Texts	Entertain the reader, such as in most fictional texts.	Kate DiCamillo, the author of *Because of Winn Dixie*, entertains her readers with the story of a young girl named Opal and the stray dog who teaches Opal the meaning of friendship.

Authors usually write to entertain, to inform, or to persuade their readers. The organization structure or pattern they use is related to what the author's purpose is. It is important to choose the pattern that best presents the information, as not all patterns will work for every piece of writing.

EXAMPLE

Read the following sentence. State the author's point in writing the sentence, whether it is to inform, persuade, express an opinion, or entertain:

> The rollercoaster reached a peak and paused for a second, before gliding down the other side of the hill with a roar.

The purpose of the sentence is to entertain the reader. The author does not state his or her opinion on the topic, and the sentence doesn't inform the reader about an important topic. The sentence does not persuade the reader to accept a certain point of view, and is instead meant to entertain the reader by giving them the feeling they might get from riding an exciting roller coaster.

Notice that the text describes an event, rather than an issue or conflict. The event is part of a larger tale, where a series of events occur to form an entire story. The reader may notice that the author uses descriptive words to present the setting, such as gliding and roar. The reader can better picture a story when the setting is clearly presented.

PRINT AND GRAPHIC FEATURES

An author may show information in a chart, a graph, in paragraph format, or as a list. Information may also be shown in a picture or a diagram. The way an author chooses to show information is often based on the purpose of the text and the audience that the text is meant to reach.

A reader may be asked to answer questions based on the graphic by itself, how the graphic relates to the text, or how the text would best be shown in a graphic form. Some common examples of graphics are cause and effect organizers, circle graphs, bar graphs, illustrations, and diagrams.

CAUSE AND EFFECT GRAPHIC ORGANIZERS

Cause-and-effect graphic organizers are often used to map the **elements of a story**. A reader might read a story about a string of events and then be asked to correctly fill in either the **cause** or **effect** of an event in the story.

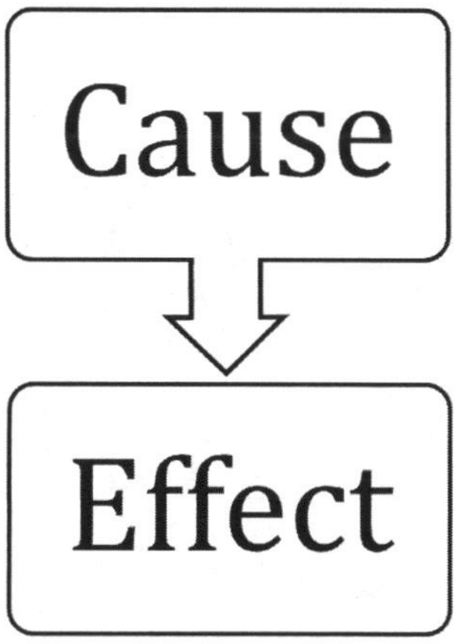

EXAMPLE

Read the following excerpt from *Ramona Quimby, Age 8* by Beverly Cleary and decide what the cause of the hectic morning at the Quimby house is.

> With all four members of the family leaving at different times in different directions, mornings were flurried in the Quimby household.

A **cause and effect** graphic organizer for this excerpt might look something like this:

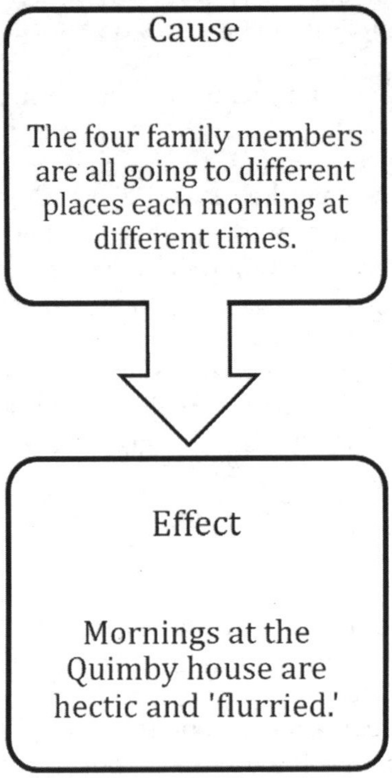

Circle Graphs

Circle graphs, also called pie charts, are often used to represent information that can be shown as **parts of a whole**. For example, this graph shows the results of people being asked about their favorite color:

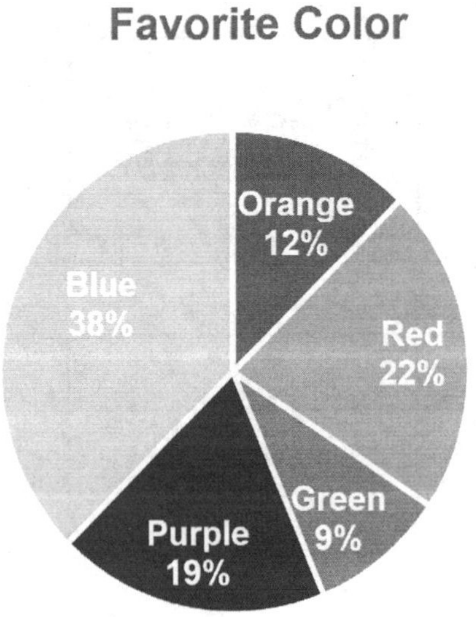

BAR GRAPHS

Bar graphs are used to show information about **numbers**. For example, this graph is a different way of representing the same results as those in the circle graph.

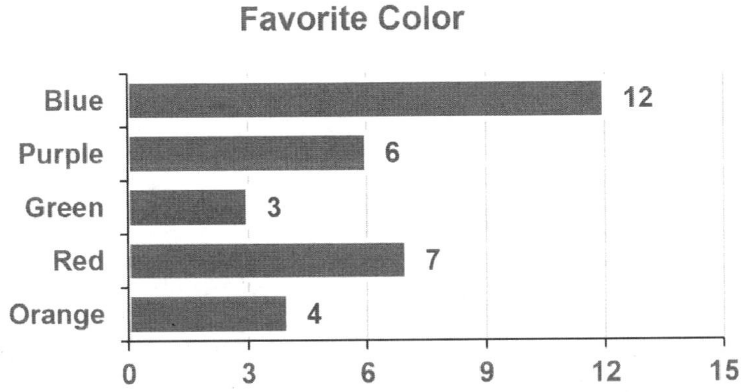

ILLUSTRATIONS AND PHOTOGRAPHS

Authors may choose to include **illustrations** or **photographs** (or both) with their texts. These two image types both show something from the text or give more information about the text.

Illustrations are drawings of an object. They may be based on reality, or they may represent an artist's abstract idea. For example, this is an illustration of a 1903 automobile:

Photographs are pictures of objects. They are generally extremely realistic, and most often show an object as it actually existed at that moment in time. For example, this is a photograph of a 1917 automobile:

Both illustrations and photographs give the reader another way to relate to and understand the text. The reader may be asked how the image relates to the text, what type of caption the image should be given, or why the author chose to include the image with the text.

DIAGRAMS

Diagrams are used to show information in a visual way. There are many different types of diagrams, including:

Diagrams that show the parts of an object, how they work together, or how they should be put together. This is an example of a diagram which shows how gears turn together

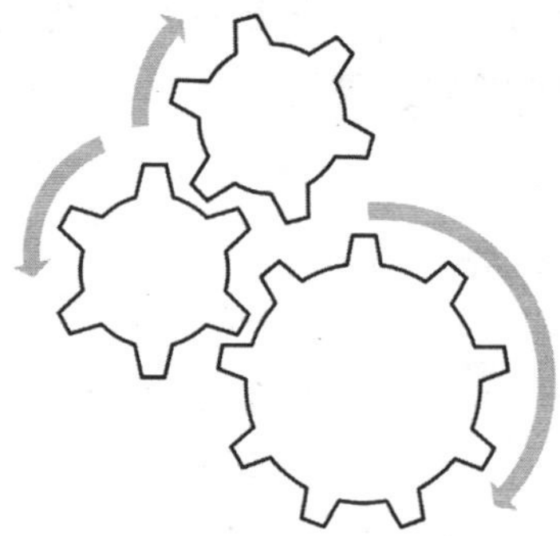

Diagrams that show how information is related are called **Venn Diagrams**. These are ways to visually see the way in which two different ideas overlap. This is an example of a Venn Diagram comparing cats and dogs:

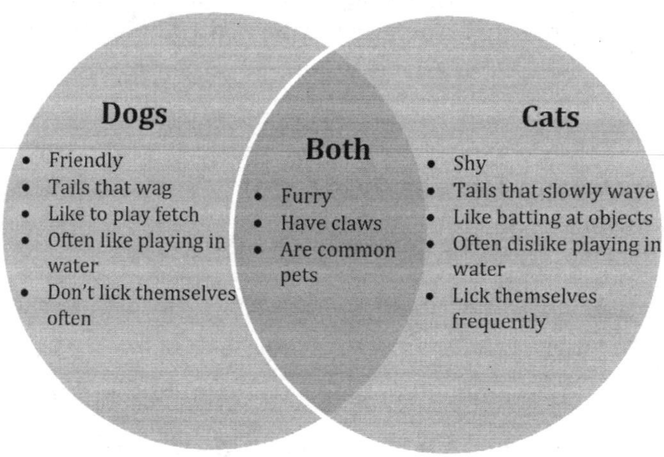

LITERAL AND FIGURATIVE LANGUAGE

Many types of text use both **literal language**, which means just what it says, and **figurative language**, which means something more than the literal words being used.

Figurative language is a literary device that allows the author to expand reality in a vivid way. When an author uses figurative language, she connects things in an exaggerated way in order to create a memorable image, or **imagery**, which helps to describe a situation in a new way for the reader. Authors try to tap into the senses to help their reader "see" what they are describing. Some common forms of figurative language include:

	Definition	Example
Metaphor	Puts one idea in place of another to draw a parallel between the two ideas.	An author might write "Her room was a pigsty," to compare a person's bedroom to a dirty spot where pigs sleep.
Simile	Shows similarity between two ideas or objects, using the words "like" or "as."	An author might write "The princess is as beautiful as a rose" to compare the appearance of a woman to a beautiful flower.
Hyperbole	An extreme exaggeration of an idea.	A character says "I'm starving to death!" to show that they are really hungry. Most of the time a character who says this is not literally going to die from hunger, they are just ready for a snack.
Irony	Uses sarcasm or humor (usually with an emphasis on the opposite) to show difference from literal meaning.	A character says "Well today must be my lucky day!" after they left their homework on the kitchen table, they are being ironic. The irony used here helps show that it is definitely *not* the character's lucky day.
Personification	Gives life or human characteristics to an inanimate object.	An author writes "The trees whispered to each other across the wide blue sky," they are using personification to help the reader imagine the scene. Trees are not human beings, so they do not whisper, but the image created in the reader stands out more than a literal description would.

Review Video: Figurative Language
Visit mometrix.com/academy and enter code: 584902

Sound Devices

Sound devices allow authors to add another level to their texts by tapping into the spoken part of language. Authors may use many sound devices to create meaning and help readers understand them better, including:

Onomatopoeia

- Appeals to the reader's sense of hearing by using words that copy the noises objects or people make, like sound effects.
- For example, an author might write "The soccer ball whooshed across the field into the goalie's net, scoring the winning point!" The word "whooshed" is an **onomatopoeia** because it mimics the sound of air moving quickly. Because the writer chose to include an onomatopoeia, the reader is able to better picture the action in the sentence.

Alliteration, Assonance, and Consonance

- **Alliteration**, **assonance**, and **consonance** all deal with using the same sound throughout a line or sentence. Assonance refers to alliteration with a repeated vowel sound, whereas consonance refers to alliteration with consonant sounds.
- For example, the following line contains two sets of alliteration: "I saw a fly fly past my eye, straight into a fresh cherry pie. I felt a flea flee away from my knee and onto the sleeping dog." The first line uses the same sound in the words *I, fly, eye,* and *pie,* which is assonance. The second line uses both assonance and consonance, using the same vowel sound in *flea, flee, knee,* and, *sleeping*. The repeated consonants show up in the words *felt, flea*, and *flee.*

Point of View

Authors choose which character tells the story they are writing. This is called **point of view**. The point of view affects the story in many ways. There are three general types of point of view:

First Person

- Tells a story through the eyes of one character.
- Uses the pronouns 'I,' 'me,' 'we,' and 'my.'
- The reader gets only one side of the story, without any other angles on what may have happened in the text

Second Person

- Tells a story using the pronoun 'you.'
- The least common point of view.

Third Person

- Tells a story about a character or group of characters from an outside viewpoint.
- Uses the words 'her', 'his,' 'they,' or a name to talk about a character or characters.
- A common way to show action in a story which allows the author to easily and realistically tell a story from more than one person's viewpoint.
- Gives readers a more complete view of a story as it is told from many different perspectives.

Style and Voice

Style and voice play an important role in the development of a story. The reader's impression of a story can vary based on the style and voice used by the author. **Style** refers to the way an author uses words, phrases, and sentence structure. The style of the text can change depending on whether the author uses short, choppy sentences, long, elaborate sentences, formal language, or informal language. **Voice** refers to the characteristics of a text that show the author's personality and distinguish the author from other writers. An author's voice may be recognized through the way they use words or the way they organize and present their thoughts. Voice is specific to each writer, and it can be as specific and unique as personality.

Chapter Quiz

1. An author's purpose in writing fiction is most often to:

a. Persuade
b. Inform
c. Entertain
d. Express

2. What is the least common point of view, that tells a story using the pronouns "you"?

a. First person
b. Second person
c. Third person
d. Narrator

3. What type of graphic can be used to visually see the way in which two different ideas overlap?

a. Circle graph
b. Bar graph
c. Venn diagram
d. Cause and effect organizer

4. What common form of figurative language puts one idea in place of another to draw a parallel between the two ideas?

a. Metaphor
b. Simile
c. Hyperbole
d. Irony

5. What sound device appeals to the reader's sense of hearing by using words that copy the noises objects or people make (for example, pow or whoosh)?

a. Onomatopoeia
b. Alliteration
c. Assonance
d. Consonance

Chapter Quiz Answer Key

1. C: See section **Author's Purpose**

2. B: See section **Second Person**

3. C: See section **Diagrams**

4. A: See section **Metaphor**

5. A: See section **Onomatopoeia**

Writing

Spelling

Vowels and Consonants

Vowels and consonants describe the sounds in the English language. **Vowels** are the sounds made with only the voice, such as /a/, /e/, /i/, /o/, and /u/. Sometimes the letter y can make an /i/ sound. Consonants make up all of the other sounds in English. Consonants are sounded out by using the tongue, teeth, and lips.

Syllables

Syllables are the individual sounds that make up spoken words. Syllables can be determined by saying a word out loud and listening to what the individual sounds are. Some people split sounds up differently, but the important part of syllables is knowing where each sound in a word starts and stops.

One Syllable	Two Syllable	Three Syllable	Four Syllable
Bat	Draw-ing	Ba-tter-y	Com-for-ta-ble
Car	Foot-ball	Com-put-er	In-vis-i-ble
Home	Wa-ter	Flam-in-go	Wat-er-mel-on

Sometimes, words are diagrammed using the letters v and c to describe the vowels and consonants in the word. This helps to determine what types of syllables the word contains.

	Closed Syllables	Open Syllables	VCe Syllables
Word	Cat	Banana	Ripe
Pronunciation	/Kat/	/Buh-Na-Nuh/	/Rīp/
Syllables	CVC	CV-CV-CV	CVC

Notice how in the first example, cat is one syllable, which is made up of a consonant sound from the letter c, a vowel from the letter a, and another consonant sound from the letter t. In the second example, banana is three syllables, each of which has a consonant followed by a vowel.

Closed Syllables

Closed syllables are the easiest to recognize. They are marked by a consonant sound closing off the beginning or end of a syllable.

Open Syllables

Open syllable refers to the beginning or end of a syllable that does not have a consonant closing it off. Examples of this include the words *egg* and *blue*. The number and placement of consonants in different open syllables can affect the way the vowel is pronounced in each syllable.

	VCCV	VCV
Word	Tennis, Method	Robin, Tiger
Pronunciation	/Ten-is/, /Meth-od /	/Rob-in/, /Tī-ger/
Syllables	VC/CV, VCC/V	VC/V, V/CV

VCe Syllables

VCe syllables refer to words that have a silent e in them. The letter e is included to help identify the word when reading it, but the e sound is not spoken. Examples of words with silent e sounds are *bite*, *cake*, *flute*, and *tube*.

VV Syllables

When two vowels appear next to each other in a word, they may work together to make a single sound. However, when the vowels do not make one sound together, they mark the end of one syllable and the beginning of another syllable. These are VV syllables, also called vowel teams. For example, *duel*, *flour*, and *diary* all contain VV syllables.

R-Controlled Vowel Syllables

R-controlled syllables are formed when an *r* comes after a vowel. In r-controlled syllables, the vowel is paired with the *r* and makes a unique sound. Examples of words with r-controlled syllables are *jar*, *teacher*, *fir*, *torn*, and *spur*.

Final Stable Syllables

When a word ends in a Cle syllable, or a consonant followed by *le*, it has a final stable syllable. The syllable is made of these three letters. Examples of words with final stable syllables are *spectacle*, *thimble*, and *giggle*.

Homophones

Homophones are words that sound the same when spoken aloud, but which have different definitions. **Homophones** are usually spelled differently. Below is a list of common homophones.

Word 1	Word 2	Word 3
Allowed	Aloud	
Ate	Eight	
Be	Bee	
Blew	Blue	
Board	Bored	
Cell	Sell	
Dear	Deer	
Eye	I	
Here	Hear	
Hour	Our	
Its	It's	
Knot	Not	

Word 1	Word 2	Word 3
Night	Knight	
Mail	Male	
Pair	Pear	Pare
Plane	Plain	
Right	Write	
Road	Rode	
Some	Sum	
Sun	Son	
There	Their	They're
Two	To	Too
Way	Weigh	
Week	Weak	
Whole	Hole	

COMMONLY MISSPELLED HOMOPHONES

TO, TOO, AND TWO

To can be an adverb or a preposition for showing direction, purpose, and relationship. A dictionary can also be used to see the many other ways to use *to* in a sentence.

Examples: I went to the store. | I want to go with you.

Too is an adverb that means *also, as well, very,* or *in excess.*

Examples: I can walk a mile too. | You have eaten too much.

Two is a number.

Example: You have two minutes left.

THERE, THEIR, AND THEY'RE

There can be an adjective, adverb, or pronoun. Often, *there* is used to show a place or to start a sentence.

Examples: I went there yesterday. | There is something in his pocket.

Their is a pronoun that is used to show ownership.

Examples: He is their father. | This is their fourth apology this week.

They're is a contraction of *they are.*

Example: Did you know that they're in town?

KNEW AND NEW

Knew is the past tense of *know.*

Example: I knew the answer.

New is an adjective that means something is current, has not been used, or is modern.

Example: This is my new phone.

Its and It's

Its is a possessive pronoun that shows ownership.

Example: The guitar is in its case.

It's is a contraction of *it is*.

Example: It's an honor and a privilege to meet you.

Your and You're

Your is a pronoun that shows ownership.

Example: This is your moment to shine.

You're is a contraction of *you are*.

Example: Yes, you're correct.

Example

In the passage below, choose the correctly spelled word from each pair in parentheses.

> My grandparents gave me a (knew/new) raincoat when I visited them yesterday. It was the perfect gift because it started raining when I left (their/there) house! The rain was very heavy, but the raincoat kept me (drie/dry) and warm. When I got home, I wrote and mailed them a letter to thank them for (their/thier) useful gift.

The first set of words is *knew* and *new*. Remember that homophones are words that are spelled differently but sound the same when spoken out loud. These words have different meanings, so it is important to choose the correct homophone carefully. In this sentence, the word is being used to describe a raincoat, so it must be an adjective. *Knew* is the past tense form of the verb *know*, while *new* is an adjective. *New* is the correct choice for the first set of words.

The next set of words is *their* and *there*. This is another set of homophones! Remember what each spelling means. *There* is most commonly used to show location, and *their* is a possessive pronoun. How is the word used in the sentence? It comes before *house* and tells who the house belongs to. Since *their* is used to show ownership, it is the correct choice in this set.

The third set of words is *drie* and *dry*. One of these words is spelled correctly, while the other is not. Remember that every word must have at least one vowel, and *y* can sometimes act as a vowel. There is not always a rule for when a word should end in *ie* or *y*, so this is an example of a word that should be memorized. *Dry* is the correct spelling.

The final set of words is their and thier. Remember the rule for spelling words that use *e* and *i* together. In this set, there is no *c* and the vowels do not make a long *a* sound together. The *i* must come before the *e* in this case, so *their* is the correct choice.

Compound Words

Compound words are when two simple words are used together to create a new word.

First Word	Second Word	Compound Word
Apple	Sauce	Applesauce
Base	Ball	Baseball
Butter	Fly	Butterfly
Cup	Cake	Cupcake
Good	Night	Goodnight
Jelly	Fish	Jellyfish
Rain	Bow	Rainbow
Water	Melon	Watermelon

Contractions

Contractions are shortened versions of two words which are commonly used together. Contractions should generally be avoided in formal writing.

First Word	Second Word	Contraction
Are	Not	Aren't
Can	Not	Can't
Could	Not	Couldn't
Did	Not	Didn't
Have	Not	Haven't
Is	Not	Isn't
I	Am	I'm
I	Will	I'll
I	Have	I've
Let	Us	Let's
They	Will	They'll

Abbreviations

Abbreviations are shortened forms of complicated or commonly used words.

Category	Full Word	Abbreviation
Days of the Week	Sunday	Sun.
	Monday	Mon.
	Tuesday	Tues.
	Wednesday	Wed.
	Thursday	Thurs.
	Friday	Fri.
	Saturday	Sat.
Months	January	Jan.
	February	Feb.
	March	Mar.
	April	Apr.
	May	May – no abbreviation
	June	Jun.
	July	Jul.
	August	Aug
	September	Sept.
	October	Oct.
	November	Nov.
	December	Dec.
Places	Apartment	Apt.
	Street	St.
	Avenue	Ave.
	Road	Rd.
People	Mister	Mr.
	Missus	Mrs.
	Miss	Ms.
	Senior	Sr.
	Junior	Jr.
	Doctor	Dr.
Measurements	Inches	In.
	Centimeters	cm.
	Foot/feet	ft.

Affixes and Root Words

Affixes are syllables attached to the beginning or end of a word to adjust its meaning. Both prefixes and suffixes are affixes. A **prefix** is a syllable that appears at the beginning of a word that adjusts the root, or base, word' s meaning. For example, the prefix *mis* means wrong. When combined with the root word *spelling*, the word *misspelling* is created, which means wrong spelling. A **root word** is the base of a word that can have affixes added to it. For example, the suffix *-er* can be added to the root word *manage* to create *manager*, which means a person or thing who manages. The suffix *-able*, meaning capable of, can be added to *manage* to create *managable*, which means capable of being managed. Keep in mind that not every prefix and suffix can be simply added to a root word, since adding an affix will sometimes require some other spelling changes for the root word.

Common Prefixes

Prefix	Definition	Examples
anti-	against, opposing	antigravity, antidote
com-	with, together, very	community, combine
de-	from	depart, detangle
dis-	away, off, down, not	dislike, disappear
ex-	out	extract, exterior
inter-	among, between	intersection, interstate
mis-	bad, poorly, not	mistake, misspell, misunderstand
non-	not	nonexistent, nonsense
over-	above, in excess	overdone, overhead
post-	after, following	postpone, postscript
pre-	before, previous	prevent, premade
pro-	forward, in place of	propel, pronoun
retro-	back, backward	retrospect, retrograde
semi-	half, partly	semicircle, semicolon
sub-	under, beneath	submarine, subject
super-	above, extra	superstore, supervise
re-	backward, again	repeat, redo
trans-	across, beyond, over	transform, transport, transit
un-	not, reverse of	unhappy, unlock
uni-	one	uniform, unity

Common Suffixes

Suffix	Definition	Examples
-able or -ible	capable of being	suitable, edible
-ation	action, state, result	occupation, federation, starvation
-dom	state, rank, condition	kingdom, wisdom
-en	cause to be, become	deepen, strengthen
-er or -or	role, function	teacher, elevator
-ess	feminine	waitress, actress
-ful	filled with, marked by	thankful, hateful
-hood	state, condition	falsehood, statehood
-ion	action, result, state	union, confusion
-ish	suggesting, like	feverish, childish
-ist	worker, status, follower	dentist, finalist, colonist
-ity or -ty	state, quality, condition	ability, faulty
-ize	cause to be, treat as	realize, emphasize
-less	lacking, without	hopeless, countless
-ment	result, action	refreshment, employment
-ness	quality, state	greatness, dullness
-ous	marked by, given to	religious, gracious
-ship	status, relationship, trait	penmanship, friendship

Spelling Changes with Suffixes

When a suffix is added to the root word, usually the resulting word is spelled just like the root word and the suffix put together. However, there are some words that will require other spelling changes when a suffix is added. These changes include doubling consonants, removing *e*, and changing *y* to *i*.

Double Consonants

Most words that end in a closed syllable with one closing consonant will need the final consonant doubled if a suffix is being added.

Adding -ing: fibbing, submitting, running

Adding -er: sadder, flipper, hummer

Adding -est: biggest, flattest, hippest

Removing E

Many words ending with a VCe syllable will lose the silent *e* when a suffix is added. This only applies if the first letter of the suffix is a vowel.

Root Words Ending in Y

If the root word ends with a consonant and a *y,* when a suffix is added, an *i* will replace the *y*.

Adding -ness: silliness, readiness, stickiness

Adding -ous: glorious, studious, industrious

Adding -ed: applied, satisfied, spied

Common Spelling Mistakes

Vowels

There must be a vowel in every word. If a writer spells a word without a vowel, he or she has made a mistake and should correct it. Not every word needs a consonant, and there are even some words that are made of one vowel, like *a* or *I*. If a word has more than one syllable, there should also be at least one vowel in every syllable. However, there are words and syllables that do not contain *a*, *e*, *i*, *o*, and *u*. In these words and syllables, *y* acts as a vowel.

I Before E

If a word contains the letters *i* and *e* right next to each other, the *i* usually goes before the *e*, such as in *relieve*. However, if the two letters come right after a *c*, then the *e* should go before the *i*, such as in *receipt*. Also, if the two letters make a long *a* sound when spoken aloud, the *e* should go before the *i*, such as in *their*. Several words do not follow these rules, so it is best to double-check the spelling of confusing words in the dictionary.

Chapter Quiz

1. Which of the following words has three syllables?

a. Invisible
b. Battery
c. Drawing
d. Football

2. When a word ends in a Cle syllable, or a consonant followed by *le* (for example, spectacle, thimble, or giggle), it has what type of syllable?

a. VCe syllable
b. VV syllable
c. Final stable syllable
d. R-controlled syllable

3. Applesauce, cupcake, and rainbow are all:

a. Compound words
b. Contractions
c. Abbreviations
d. Homophones

4. All of the following prefixes can mean "not" EXCEPT for:

a. dis-
b. ex-
c. non-
d. un-

5. When adding a suffix to most words that end in a closed syllable with one closing consonant (for example, sad or flip), what change needs to be made to the root word?

a. No change is needed
b. Add a y before the suffix
c. Add a silent e
d. Double the final consonant

6. If a word contains the letters *i* and *e* right next to each other, the *i* usually goes before the *e*, EXCEPT when the two letters come right after:

a. C
b. F
c. N
d. T

7. There, they're, and their are commonly misspelled homophones. Which one is a pronoun that is used to show ownership?

a. There
b. They're
c. Their
d. All of the above

Chapter Quiz Answer Key

1. B: See section **Syllables**

2. C: See section **Final Stable Syllables**

3. A: See section **Compound Words**

4. B: See section **Common Prefixes**

5. D: See section **Double Consonants**

6. A: See section **I Before E**

7. C: See section **There, Their, and They're**

Writing Process

Brainstorming

When choosing what to write about, activities like brainstorming can help inspire new ideas or help writers see how their ideas go together. **Brainstorming** means considering a variety of topics or ideas and is mainly used to find a creative approach to a subject or problem. A good first step in brainstorming is simple **free-association** with a topic. One way of doing this is sitting down with paper and pen and writing every thought that comes to mind about the topic in a word or phrase. It does not matter how helpful or good the thought seems at first; the writer should write down everything that comes to mind about the topic. Then, the writer should read the list over a few times. Next, he or she should look for patterns, repetitions, and clusters of ideas. This allows a variety of fresh ideas to come as the writer thinks about the topic.

Free Writing

Free writing is a more organized form of brainstorming. **Free writing** means taking a limited amount of time, like 2 to 3 minutes, to write everything that comes to mind about a topic in complete sentences. When the time is up, the writer should review everything he or she has written down. Many of the sentences may not make sense, but they may contain ideas and details that help the writer organize his or her ideas and prepare to plan the composition. Usually, free writing results in more useful ideas than brainstorming because the writer's thoughts and connections are written in complete sentences. However, both methods can be used together to help the writer prepare to plan and write a composition.

Mapping

One specific way to use graphic organizers is to map an essay. There are many different types of graphic organizers. One easy method to create one is to draw a circle in the middle of the page and write a broad topic in it. Then, draw smaller circles with related topics and ideas, or with topics that fit within the broad topic, written inside and draw line to connect each circle to the main circle. This method can show ideas that fit within the broad topic and will help guide the essay, or it can show which ideas may work better as the main topic of the essay.

Once the main idea and other ideas and details for the essay have been chosen, they can be used to map the essay. Mapping is another word for using a certain type of graphic organizer. These graphic organizers look like a map and organize ideas and details as they will appear in the essay. The essay map can have the main idea at the top or in the center. If the main idea is at the top, the supporting ideas will appear below it in a row, and any additional details will appear under the supporting idea they go with. If the main idea appears in the center, the supporting ideas may appear around it, and the additional details will appear around the supporting ideas they go with.

Planning

Planning is the process of organizing a piece of writing before writing a draft. At the beginning of planning, writers should decide **why they are writing** and **who will read what they write**. The writer must also choose a **genre**, which is the **type** of composition he or she will write. There are fiction genres, such as comedy, folklore, action, and mystery. There are also nonfiction genres, such as essays, reports, poems, and journals. To plan his or her composition, a writer may create an outline or a graphic organizer, such as a Venn diagram, a spider-map, or a flowchart. These methods should help the writer choose their topic, main ideas, and how to organize the composition. If the writer needs to do research for the composition, he or she may also do so as they plan. Planning helps writers organize all of their ideas and decide if they have enough information to begin their first draft. However, writers should remember that the decisions they make during planning may change later, so their plan does not have to be perfect.

DRAFTING

Writers may then use their plan, outline, or graphic organizer to compose their first draft. They may write more drafts after the first one to improve their writing. Writing multiple drafts can help writers think of different ways to state their ideas and correct mistakes that may be hard to fix without rewriting a section of the composition, or the whole composition. There is no "right" number of drafts, so different writers may write a different number of drafts. Writing drafts also makes it easier to write freely because a writer can improve his or her composition with each draft they write.

REVISING, EDITING, AND PROOFREADING

Once a writer completes a draft, he or she can move on to revising, editing, and proofreading to improve the draft. **Revising** is making sure that the composition is right for the audience, is not missing important information, is on topic, and is well organized. Revising may happen after the first draft so that errors are not repeated in the next draft. Each draft should be revised before the next one is written so that no mistakes are missed. **Editing** comes next. Editing a composition includes steps like improving transitions between paragraphs and making sure each paragraph is on topic. While editing, the writer must pay attention to the words he or she uses and the way the information in each paragraph is organized. Writers may also fix grammar mistakes in the editing phase, since some errors will require a writer to rewrite large parts of their work. **Proofreading** means fixing misspelled words, errors in grammar, and any other small mistakes in the composition.

During the revising, editing, and proofreading steps, it can be helpful for writers to ask a peer to read their work, since he or she may notice mistakes or problems the writer missed before. A writer may also choose to read his or her own work aloud, or listen to someone else read it. Hearing a composition aloud can help writers find mistakes or opportunities for improvement in their work more easily. This happens because when something is read aloud, the person reading the text must pay closer attention to the words on the page. When a writer or a peer reads the composition, they should point out any sentence that confuses them the first time they read it. Most of these sentences can be revised in a way that makes it easier to read and understand.

ADDING AND REMOVING INFORMATION

While both revising and editing may involve changing the words in a composition, they can also involve adding or taking away words. When a writer has completed a draft and reread it, he or she may notice that something, such as a transition, important details, or an explanatory sentence, is missing. Simply changing the words to make the passage sound better will not solve this problem, so the writer must **add** whatever words and information is needed to make the passage make sense and achieve the writer's purpose.

In other cases, a writer may have words, a sentence, or sometimes an entire paragraph that gives unnecessary information or explains the information in a way that is confusing. When this happens, the extra words and information weaken the composition and must be **removed**. Sometimes, this is difficult for writers to do because it may require them to remove writing they are proud of or a fact they find interesting. Despite this, revising and editing are steps meant to improve and strengthen a composition, so the writer should change, add, or remove parts of his or her writing in a way that makes it better and achieves his or her purpose.

Revising Sentences

Sentence variety is important to consider when writing an essay. A variety of sentence lengths and types can make an essay more engaging, and different types of sentences can sometimes help readers better understand information. For example, a sentence containing a list may make more sense when written with a simple sentence structure, since writing a compound sentence containing a list may give the reader too much information at once. On the other hand, information that is closely related and can be connected with a conjunction should be written in a compound sentence, rather than a simple sentence, since a compound sentence helps the reader see that the information goes together.

Using only simple sentences often makes writing boring and bothersome to read. Writing using only compound sentences makes it difficult for writers to explain information well and difficult for readers to understand, since every sentence will include a coordinating conjunction. To check an essay for sentence variety, it is helpful to look at whether the essay contains different sentence structures and lengths. It is also important to pay attention to the way each sentence starts and avoid beginning with the same words or phrases.

Revising Vocabulary

When writing informational or argumentative texts, it is important to use **precise vocabulary**, or **word choice**, to explain your main idea and supporting details. Generalized vocabulary will not help the audience fully understand the points that you are attempting to make because it will not accurately explain your main idea and supporting details. Precise vocabulary is important to use because it will accurately describe the ideas that are central to your text. When you research a subject, make sure to familiarize yourself with any vocabulary that is involved in its explanation. Use context clues, dictionaries, or, if necessary, a technical dictionary to decode any words that you are not familiar with. Precise vocabulary also impacts the effectiveness of narrative text. Carefully choosing vocabulary to describe sensory details, or imagery, helps writers paint the best possible picture of the events they are describing through their writing.

Chapter Quiz

1. Which of the following means taking a limited amount of time, like 2 to 3 minutes, to write everything that comes to mind about a topic in complete sentences?

a. Brainstorming
b. Drafting
c. Mapping
d. Free writing

2. What is often the first step after a writer completes a draft, and involves making sure that the composition is right for the audience, it is not missing important information, is on topic, and is well organized?

a. Adapting
b. Editing
c. Proofreading
d. Revising

3. When revising sentences in an essay, which of the following is NOT good advice?

a. Avoid beginning sentences with the same words or phrases
b. Include a variety of sentence lengths
c. Improve understanding by only using compound sentences
d. Keep sentences simple when they include lists

4. In what step of the writing process does the writer decide why they are writing, who will read what they write, and what genre they want to write?

a. Brainstorming
b. Drafting
c. Mapping
d. Planning

Chapter Quiz Answer Key

1. D: See section **Free Writing**

2. D: See section **Revising, Editing, and Proofreading**

3. C: See section **Revising Sentences**

4. D: See section **Planning**

Essay Structure and Organization

Controlling Ideas and Supporting Details

In the first paragraph of a composition, writers include a sentence that explains the **controlling idea.** The rest of the paragraph shows the reader why the topic of the essay is interesting and includes details that support the controlling idea. One way to understand the relationship between the controlling idea and supporting information is to think about a table: the tabletop is the controlling idea, and each of the table's legs is a supporting detail or group of details. All of the legs work together to support the tabletop and create a table, just like the supporting details work together to support the controlling idea and create a composition.

Introduction

The introduction is used to capture the reader's attention and announce the essay's controlling idea. Normally, the introduction contains about 3-5 sentences. An introduction can begin with an interesting quote, a question, a strong opinion, or something else that will **interest** the reader's and prompt them to keep reading. If the composition has a prompt, the introduction should **restate** or **summarize** some part of the prompt so that the reader will have an idea of what information will be in the essay. Finally, your introduction should include the **controlling idea**, the primary thing the essay will tell the reader.

Review Video: Introduction
Visit mometrix.com/academy and enter code: 961328

Body

In an essay's introduction, the writer states the controlling idea and prepares the reader for the information in the rest of the composition. In the body of the composition, the writer **explains**, **demonstrates**, and **gives more information about** the **controlling idea**. This is done using supporting details and examples that are relevant to the controlling idea of the composition. For example, if the composition's controlling idea is a vacation the writer took, the body will include descriptions of where the writer went, what they experienced, and what they thought of the trip. If the composition's controlling idea is the writer's opinion, the body will include examples and facts that show why he or she has formed that opinion. If composition's controlling idea is a topic and the writer wants to instruct the reader, the body will contain facts, explanations, and examples that help teach the reader about the controlling idea. A writer will use supporting details to explain the controlling idea throughout the body.

The body should also contain multiple paragraphs, and the order the writer puts these paragraphs in is important. Each paragraph should include at least one supporting detail, but a paragraph may include more than one if two or more supporting details work together to support the controlling idea. If the controlling idea is to describe something that happened, the paragraphs should match the order in which the events occurred. If the controlling idea is to present an opinion or instruct the reader, the paragraphs should be ordered in the way that would make the most sense to the reader. The order of body paragraphs is important because it can impact how easy a composition is to read.

Review Video: Drafting Body Paragraphs
Visit mometrix.com/academy and enter code: 724590

Paragraphs

After the introduction of a passage, the body paragraphs will explain and elaborate upon the controlling idea. While each paragraph should relate to the controlling idea of the composition, each paragraph should focus on one point or supporting detail. Normally, a paragraph has a good topic sentence that summarizes the paragraph's main point. A topic sentence is a sentence that gives an introduction to the paragraph and its contents. Topic sentences should contain information that is more specific than what is in the introduction and may include a supporting detail, but they should not contain explanations or examples.

Supporting Details

The next sentences in the paragraph should support the topic sentence. These sentences can contain examples, explanations, or other specific information that supports the topic sentence, which supports the controlling idea of the composition. While a paragraph may be structured in any way, as long as it logically provides information that supports the controlling idea, it can be best to use a template or pattern to make sure that each paragraph is complete and well organized. For example, a good template to follow is topic sentence, evidence, explanation, conclusion. This means that after the topic sentence, the next sentence should provide evidence, such as a quote or example, that shows that the supporting detail is true or relevant. Next, the paragraph should include a sentence that explains how the evidence supports the paragraph's main point. If there are multiple examples or quotes, more than one sentence may be used for each section. Finally, there should be a sentence that concludes the paragraph. The concluding sentence may be similar to the topic sentence, but it should help the reader understand the paragraph and prepare them for the next one.

Length of a Paragraph

A paragraph must contain enough information to support its main point and the composition's controlling idea. A paragraph of two or three sentences will most likely not support the main point or controlling idea because it is not likely to contain enough information, explanation, or evidence. When a paragraph does not support the main point or controlling idea, it does not help the writer achieve their purpose or goal for writing the essay. A helpful, informative paragraph will often have somewhere from three to five sentences.

Starting a New Paragraph

For most forms of writing, you will need to use multiple paragraphs. This means that deciding when to start a new paragraph is very important. Reasons for starting a new paragraph include:

- To separate the introduction and conclusion from the body paragraphs
- To move from one supporting detail or point to another
- To indicate an important shift in time or place
- To show a comparison, contrast, or cause and effect relationship

Transitions

Transitions between sentences and paragraphs guide readers from idea to idea and show relationships between sentences and paragraphs. Writers should use transitions carefully and only when they are truly helpful. They should also be selected to fit the author's purpose. Transitions can show relationships such as time, comparison, an order of events, and cause and effect. Transitions are often used at the beginning of a phrase, sentence, or paragraph, since this helps prepare the reader for the next piece of information.

Types of Transitional Words

Time	Afterward, immediately, earlier, meanwhile, recently, lately, now, since, soon, when, then, until, before, etc.
Sequence	too, first, second, further, moreover, also, again, and, next, still, besides, finally
Comparison	similarly, in the same way, likewise, also, again, once more
Contrasting	but, although, despite, however, instead, nevertheless, on the one hand... on the other hand, regardless, yet, in contrast.
Cause and Effect	because, consequently, thus, therefore, then, to this end, since, so, as a result, if... then, accordingly
Examples	for example, for instance, such as, to illustrate, indeed, in fact, specifically
Place	near, far, here, there, to the left/right, next to, above, below, beyond, opposite, beside
Repetition, Summary, or Conclusion	as mentioned earlier, as noted, in other words, in short, on the whole, to summarize, therefore, as a result, to conclude, in conclusion
Addition	and, also, furthermore, moreover

Review Video: <u>Transition Words</u>
Visit mometrix.com/academy and enter code: 707563

Conclusion

The conclusion of a composition should summarize the controlling idea and show that it has been explained well. A good conclusion shows the reader why the author's controlling idea is meaningful and important and how the supporting details should help the reader understand the controlling idea. The conclusion should also give the reader something to think about that is related to the controlling idea. For example, in the conclusion, the author can invite readers to think about how they feel or what they think after reading the composition. Some things to avoid when writing conclusions include:

- Introducing a completely new idea
- Apologizing for one's opinions or writing
- Repeating the controlling idea word for word rather than summarizing them
- Using the conclusion to summarize every detail in the composition

Review Video: Drafting Conclusions
Visit mometrix.com/academy and enter code: 209408

Chapter Quiz

1. "Too," "and," "next," "still," "besides," and "finally" are all what type of transitional word?

a. Time
b. Sequence
c. Comparison
d. Contrasting

2. Which of the following should be avoided in an essay conclusion?

a. Reminding the reader of the central idea by repeating it word for word
b. Showing the reader why the author's central idea is meaningful and important
c. Showing that the central idea has been explained well
d. Giving the reader something to think about that is related to the central idea

3. A helpful, informative paragraph will often have how many sentences?

a. One to three sentences
b. Three to five sentences
c. Five to ten sentences
d. Ten to fifteen sentences

4. The body of an essay should do all of the following, EXCEPT:

a. Introduce the central idea
b. Demonstrate the central idea
c. Explain the central idea
d. Give information about the central idea

Chapter Quiz Answer Key

1. B: See section **Types of Transitional Words**

2. A: See section **Conclusion**

3. B: See section **Length of a Paragraph**

4. A: See section **Body**

Grammar

Subjects and Predicates

Subjects

Every sentence needs a subject and a predicate. The **subject** of a sentence names who or what the sentence is about. The subject may be directly stated in a sentence, or the subject may be implied. The **complete subject** includes the simple subject and any **modifiers**, such as adjectives, articles, prepositions, and adverbs, that go with it. To find the complete subject, ask *Who* or *What* before the verb to complete the question. The answer, including any modifiers, is the complete subject. To find the **simple subject**, remove all of the modifiers in the complete subject.

Examples:

simple subject

The small, red car is the one that he wants for Christmas.

complete subject

simple subject

The young artist is coming over for dinner.

complete subject

Review Video: Subjects in English
Visit mometrix.com/academy and enter code: 444771

An imperative sentence is a sentence that gives someone instructions or makes a request to someone. In **imperative** sentences, the verb's subject is understood, but is not actually present in the sentence. For example, this about the sentence *Drive to the store*. This sentence is a command, and the subject is *you*. If the subject were directly stated, the sentence would be *You, drive to the store*. Another fact to consider is that, normally, the subject comes before the verb. However, the subject comes after the verb in sentences that begin with *There are* or *There was*.

Direct:

John knows the way to the park.	Who knows the way to the park?	John
The cookies need ten more minutes.	What needs ten minutes?	The cookies
By five o'clock, Bill will need to leave.	Who needs to leave?	Bill
There are five letters on the table for him.	What is on the table?	Five letters
There were coffee and doughnuts in the house.	What was in the house?	Coffee and doughnuts

Implied:

Go to the post office for me.	Who is going to the post office?	You
Come and sit with me, please?	Who needs to come and sit?	You

Predicates

In a sentence, there is always a predicate and a subject. The subject tells what the sentence is about, and the **predicate** explains or describes the subject.

Think about the sentence *He sings*. In this sentence, we have a subject, *He*, and a predicate, *sings*. This is all that is needed for a sentence to be complete. Most sentences contain more information, but if this is all the information that is given in a sentence, then it is a complete sentence.

Now, let's look at another sentence: *John and Jane sing on Tuesday nights at the dance hall.*

subject: John and Jane — predicate: sing on Tuesday nights at the dance hall.

John and Jane sing on Tuesday nights at the dance hall.

Subject-Verb Agreement

Verbs **agree** with their subjects in number. In other words, singular subjects need singular verbs. Plural subjects need plural verbs. **Singular** is for **one** person, place, or thing. **Plural** is for **more than one** person, place, or thing. Subjects and verbs must also share the same point of view, as in first, second, or third person.

Review Video: Subject-Verb Agreement
Visit mometrix.com/academy and enter code: 479190

Number Agreement Examples:

Single Subject and Verb: Dan (singular subject) calls (singular verb) home.

Dan is one person. So, the singular verb *calls* is needed.

Plural Subject and Verb: Dan and Bob (plural subject) call (plural verb) home.

More than one person needs the plural verb *call*.

Person Agreement Examples:

First Person: I *am* walking.

Second Person: You *are* walking.

Third Person: He *is* walking.

Complications with Subject-Verb Agreement

Words Between Subject and Verb

Words that come between the simple subject and the verb do not affect subject-verb agreement.

Examples:

The joy (singular subject) of my life returns (singular verb) home tonight.

The phrase *of my life* does not affect the verb *returns*.

singular subject / singular verb

The question that still remains unanswered is "Who are you?"

Don't let the phrase "*that still remains…*" confuse you. The subject *question* goes with the verb *is.*

Compound Subjects

A compound subject is formed when two or more nouns joined by *and*, *or*, or *nor* act together as the subject of the sentence.

Joined by And

When a compound subject is joined by *and*, it is treated as a plural subject and requires a plural verb.

Examples:

plural subject / plural verb

You and Jon are invited to come to my house.

plural subject / plural verb

The pencil and paper belong to me.

Joined by Or/Nor

For a compound subject joined by *or* or *nor*, the verb must agree in number with the part of the subject that is closest to the verb.

Examples:

subject / verb

Today or tomorrow is the day.

subject / verb

Stan or Phil wants to read the book.

subject / verb

Neither the pen nor the book is on the desk.

subject / verb

Either the blanket or pillows arrive this afternoon.

Indefinite Pronouns as Subject

An indefinite pronoun is a pronoun that does not refer to a specific noun. Different indefinite pronouns are used as a singular noun, a plural noun, or change depending on how they are used.

Always Singular

Pronouns such as *each*, *either*, *everybody*, *anybody*, *somebody*, and *nobody* are always singular. This is because these pronouns always stand in for one person, place, or thing.

Examples:

singular subject | singular verb

Each of the runners has a different bib number.

singular verb | singular subject

Is either of you ready for the game?

Note: The words *each* and *either* can also be used as adjectives. For example, *each* person is unique. When one of these adjectives modifies the subject of a sentence, it is always a singular subject.

singular subject | singular verb

Everybody grows a day older every day.

singular subject | singular verb

Anybody is welcome to bring a tent.

ALWAYS PLURAL

Pronouns such as *both*, *several*, and *many* are always plural. This is because these pronouns always stand in for more than one person, place, thing, or idea.

Examples:

plural subject | plural verb

Both of the siblings were too tired to argue.

plural subject | plural verb

Many have tried, but none have succeeded.

DEPEND ON CONTEXT

Pronouns such as *some*, *any*, *all*, *none*, *more*, and *most* can be either singular or plural depending on what they are representing in the context of the sentence.

Examples:

singular subject | singular verb

All of my dog's food was still there in his bowl.

plural subject | plural verb

By the end of the night, all of my guests were already excited about coming to my next party.

EXAMPLE

Which word should go in the blank?

Joan and Susan ____ going to the store this evening.

a. Is
b. Are
c. Am
d. Was

Try using each choice in the sentence. Choice A, *is*, forms this sentence: Joan and Susan is going to the store this evening. There are two people, Joan and Susan, who are going to the store. This makes the subject of the sentence plural. *Is* is a singular verb, meaning it does not agree with the subject and cannot be the answer.

Choice B, *are*, forms this sentence: Joan and Susan are going to the store this evening. The subject of the sentence is still plural. But *are* is a plural verb! The subject and verb agree, so *are* is the correct answer.

Choice C, *am*, forms this sentence: Joan and Susan am going to the store this evening. *Am* is a singular verb, and it is also only used in first person, when the writer or speaker is referring to themself. The subject is plural, and the sentence is in third person, so *am* is not the correct answer.

Choice D, *was*, forms this sentence: Joan and Susan was going to the store this evening. *Was* is a singular verb, so it does not agree with the plural subject in this sentence.

EXAMPLE

What is the best change to make to the following sentence?

Neither Timothy nor his sisters wants to go to the Grand Canyon this summer.

a. Remove *Neither* and *nor his sisters.*
b. Change *Grand Canyon* to *Grand Canyons.*
c. Capitalize *summer.*
d. Change *wants* to *want.*

Before looking closely at each answer choice, it is helpful to first look for any errors in the sentence. This sentence appears to have an error in subject-verb agreement. This sentence mentions more than one subject, and they are joined by the word *nor*. Remember that when a sentence contains multiple subjects joined by *or* or *nor*, the verb should agree with the subject that is closest to the verb in the sentence. In this case, *his sisters* is closest to the verb. This is a plural subject, so the verb should also be plural.

Choice A suggests removing several words to create this sentence: Timothy wants to go to the Grand Canyon this summer. While this does solve the error in subject-verb agreement, since there is only one singular subject and a singular verb, this changes the meaning of the sentence. We know from the original sentence that Timothy does not want to visit the Grand Canyon, but this new sentence says that he does. While choice A makes the sentence grammatically correct, it is not the correct answer because it changes the sentence's meaning.

Choice B suggests changing *Grand Canyon* from a singular noun to a plural noun. While the Grand Canyon is made of multiple canyons, the entire location is known as the Grand Canyon. *Grand Canyon* is also the object, and subject-verb agreement is not affected by whether the object is singular or plural. Choice B is incorrect.

Choice C suggests capitalizing *summer*. Seasons do not need to be capitalized if they are not the first word in a sentence or part of a proper noun. Capitalizing *summer* also does not resolve the error in subject-verb agreement, so choice C is incorrect.

Choice D suggests changing *wants* to *want*. Remember that in this sentence, the subject closest to the verb is *sisters*, so it is a plural noun that needs a plural verb. *Wants* is a singular verb, but *want* is a plural verb. Choice D corrects the error in subject-verb agreement without creating a new error or changing the meaning of the sentence. Choice D is correct!

COMPLEMENTS

A complement is a noun, pronoun, or adjective that is used to give more information about the subject or verb in the sentence.

DIRECT OBJECTS

A direct object is a noun or pronoun that takes or receives the **action** of a verb. A complete sentence does not need a direct object, so not all sentences will have them. When you are looking for a direct object, find the verb and ask *who* or *what*.

Examples:

I took *the blanket.*

Jane read *books.*

INDIRECT OBJECTS

An indirect object is a word or group of words that show how an action had an **influence** on someone or something. If there is an indirect object in a sentence, then you always have a direct object in the sentence. When you are looking for the indirect object, find the verb and ask *to, for, whom*, or *what*.

Examples:

We taught the old dog (indirect object) a new trick (direct object).

I gave them (indirect object) a math lesson (direct object).

Review Video: Direct and Indirect Objects
Visit mometrix.com/academy and enter code: 817385

PHRASES

A phrase is a group of words that functions as a single part of speech, usually a noun, adjective, or adverb. A **phrase** is not a complete thought, and does not contain a subject, but it adds detail or explanation to a sentence, or renames something within the sentence.

CLAUSES

A clause is a group of words that contains both a subject and a predicate (verb). There are two types of clauses: independent and dependent. An **independent clause** contains a complete thought, while a **dependent (or subordinate) clause** does not. A dependent clause includes a subject and a verb, and may also contain additional information, but it cannot stand as a complete thought without being joined to an independent clause. Dependent clauses function within sentences as adjectives, adverbs, or nouns.

Example:

I am running [independent clause] because I want to stay in shape [dependent clause].

The clause *I am running* is an independent clause: it has a subject and a verb, and it gives a complete thought. The clause *because I want to stay in shape* is a dependent clause: it has a subject and a verb, but it does not express a complete thought. This is due to the fact that it begins with *because*, which shows that there is more information needed to complete the thought. This dependent clause adds detail to the independent clause to which it is attached.

Sentence Structure

Sentence structure is based on the type and number of clauses in the sentence. Two common sentence structures are simple sentences and compound sentences:

Simple

A simple sentence has one independent clause with no dependent clauses. A simple sentence may have a **compound subject** or a **compound verb**, or both.

Examples:

Judy [single subject] watered [single verb] the lawn.

Judy and Alan [compound subject] watered [single verb] the lawn.

Judy [single subject] watered [compound verb] the lawn and pulled [compound verb] weeds.

Judy and Alan [compound subject] watered [compound verb] the lawn and pulled [compound verb] weeds.

Compound

A compound sentence has two or more independent clauses with no dependent clauses. Usually, the independent clauses are joined with a comma and a coordinating conjunction or with a semicolon.

Examples:

The time has come [independent clause], and we are ready [independent clause].

I woke up at dawn [independent clause]; the sun was just coming up [independent clause].

Review Video: Sentence Structure
Visit mometrix.com/academy and enter code: 700478

Example

What is the structure of the following sentence?

Matt did his math homework and finished his chores.

a. Simple
b. Complex
c. Compound
d. This is not a complete sentence.

One way to determine what type of sentence this is to first look for any phrases and clauses. There is a subject, *Matt*, and a predicate, *did his math homework and finished his chores*. Since all of the information in the sentence fits into one subject and one predicate, the whole sentence forms one clause. Additionally, since the clause forms a complete thought by itself, it is an independent clause. So, this sentence has exactly one independent clause and no dependent clauses. What type of sentence is made of one independent clause?

Choice A says this sentence is a simple sentence. What makes a simple sentence? Simple sentences are each made of one independent clause and contain zero dependent clauses. This matches the structure of the sentence in the question, so choice A is correct!

Choice B says this sentence is a complex sentence. A complex sentence includes a dependent clause and an independent clause. This sentence does not contain a dependent clause, so Choice B is incorrect.

Choice C says this sentence is a compound sentence. Remember that a compound sentence has at least two independent clauses and no dependent clauses. This sentence only has one independent clause, so it cannot be a compound sentence. Choice C is incorrect.

Choice D says this sentence is not a complete sentence. Since this sentence has a subject and a predicate and is a complete thought, it is a complete sentence. Choice D is incorrect.

Example

Which of the following could be added to the end of this sentence to change it from a simple sentence to a compound sentence?

I went for a walk last night.

a. Because I was not tired
b. With my sister
c. And I saw a shooting star
d. Since the weather was nice

This sentence is a simple sentence, since it contains only an independent clause. To become a compound sentence, the sentence must contain two or more independent clauses, and these independent clauses should be joined by a coordinating conjunction. So, a good way to answer this question is to find the answer choice that contains a coordinating conjunction and is an independent clause.

Choice A forms this sentence: I went for a walk last night because I was not tired. While *I was not tired* is an independent clause, it is joined by the word *because*. *Because* is not a coordinating conjunction, and it causes this choice to be a dependent clause. Choice A is incorrect.

Choice B forms this sentence: I went for a walk last night with my sister. *With my sister* is actually not a clause at all, since it does not have a subject and predicate. Choice B is a phrase, so it is incorrect.

Choice C forms this sentence: I went for a walk last night, and I saw a shooting star. Because this sentence has an independent clause followed by another independent clause with a coordinating conjunction, a comma has been added after the first clause. This also means that this sentence is a compound sentence! Choice C contains a coordinating conjunction and is an independent clause, so C is correct.

Choice D forms this sentence: I went for a walk last night since the weather was nice. While *the weather was nice* is an independent clause, it is joined by the word *since*. *Since* is not a coordinating conjunction, and it makes this choice a dependent clause. This means choice D is incorrect.

Parts of Speech

Nouns

When you talk about a person, place, thing, or idea, you are talking about a **noun**. The two main types of nouns are **common** and **proper** nouns.

Common Nouns

Common nouns are generic names for people, places, and things. Common nouns are not usually capitalized.

Examples of common nouns:

People: boy, girl, worker, manager

Places: school, bank, library, home

Things: dog, cat, truck, car

Proper Nouns

Proper nouns name specific people, places, or things. All proper nouns are capitalized.

Examples of proper nouns:

People: Abraham Lincoln, George Washington, Martin Luther King, Jr.

Places: Los Angeles, California; New York; Asia

Things: Statue of Liberty, Earth, Lincoln Memorial

Note: When referring to the planet that we live on, capitalize *Earth*. When referring to the dirt, rocks, or land, lowercase *earth*.

Singular and Plural Nouns

Singular nouns name **one** person, place, thing, or idea. **Plural nouns** name **more than one** person, place, thing, or idea. Most nouns have both a singular and plural form. Many plural nouns are spelled like the singular noun with an *-s* at the end, but this is not true for all plural nouns. Singular nouns that already end in an *s, o, ch, sh,* or *x* usually end in *-es* when they are in the plural form. Singular nouns that end in a consonant followed by the letter *y* will usually lose the *y* and end in *-ies* in the plural form, and words that end with the letter *f* or *fe* will usually lose the *f* and end in *-ves.*

Some plural nouns have much different spellings than their singular form, and some plural nouns are spelled the same as their singular form. There are more rules for spelling plural nouns, but these are the most common spelling changes.

Examples of singular nouns:

Typical nouns: dog, pencil, girl, store, hope, stingray

Nouns ending in *s, o, ch, sh,* or *x*: mass, hero, lunch, polish, fox

Nouns ending in a consonant and *y*: puppy, baby, fairy, sky

Nouns ending in *f* or *fe*: self, life, calf, hoof

Examples of plural nouns:

Typical nouns: dogs, pencils, girls, stores, hopes, stingrays

Nouns ending in *s, o, ch, sh,* or *x*: masses, heroes, lunches, polishes, foxes

Nouns ending in a consonant and *y*: puppies, babies, fairies, skies

Nouns ending in a vowel and *f* or *fe*: selves, lives, calves, hooves

COLLECTIVE NOUNS

Collective nouns are the names for a group of people, places, or things that function like singular nouns. The following are examples of collective nouns: *class, company, dozen, group, herd, team,* and *public.* Collective nouns usually require an article, such as *a, an,* and *the,* which shows that the noun is a single unit. For example, a choir is a group of singers. Even though there are many singers in a choir, the word choir describes a single group. If we refer to the members of the group, and not the group itself, it is no longer a collective noun.

Incorrect: The *choir are* going to compete nationally this year.

Correct: The *choir is* going to compete nationally this year.

Incorrect: The *members* of the choir *is* competing nationally this year.

Correct: The *members* of the choir *are* competing nationally this year.

EXAMPLE

Find the error in the following sentence.

Mary, Claudia, and Rachel each have two pet bunnys.

a. *Mary, Claudia,* and *Rachel* should all be common nouns.
b. *Bunnys* should be spelled *bunny.*
c. The subject should be *the three girls* instead of *Mary, Claudia, and Rachel.*
d. *Bunnys* should be spelled *bunnies.*

Before looking at all of the answer choices, first look at the sentence and try to find the error. The sentence has correct subject-verb agreement, and it is a complete sentence. The error is in the last word, *bunnys*. Remember that singular nouns ending in *y* are spelled differently when they are made plural. The *y* goes away and is replaced with *ies*, meaning that the plural of *bunny* is *bunnies*.

Choice A says that *Mary, Claudia, and Rachel* should really be *mary, claudia, and rachel*. This is incorrect, since *Mary*, *Claudia*, and *Rachel* are all proper nouns. Remember, proper nouns should always be capitalized. Choice A is incorrect.

Choice B says that *bunnys* should actually be the singular noun *bunny*. While *bunnys* is the error in the sentence, this solution is not correct because the sentence still has a plural object. There are six bunnies, not one bunny, so choice B is incorrect.

Choice C says the sentence should say *the three girls each have two pet bunnys*. This does not improve the sentence or resolve the spelling error at the end of the sentence. The error still remains, so choice C is incorrect.

Choice D says that *bunnys* should actually be spelled *bunnies*. This choice correctly points out the misspelling in the sentence and includes the correct spelling of the word. *Bunnies* is the correct plural form of *bunny*, so choice D is correct.

EXAMPLE

Which word or words in the following sentence should be capitalized?

My neighbor sent me a postcard from her trip to see the golden gate bridge.

a. Neighbor
b. Golden Gate Bridge
c. Sent
d. Postcard

Choice A says that *neighbor* should be capitalized. *Neighbor* is a common noun. It is not someone's name, a title, a place, or any other kind of proper noun. There is no reason for *neighbor* to be capitalized, so A is incorrect.

Choice B says that *golden gate bridge* should be capitalized. The Golden Gate Bridge is a famous bridge in California. From the sentence, it is also clear that the Golden Gate Bridge is a proper noun because the neighbor specifically went to see it, and it is an object with a title. *Golden Gate Bridge* is a proper noun, so B is correct.

Choice C says that *sent* should be capitalized. *Sent* is a verb. The only time a verb should be capitalized is when it is part of a title. In this sentence, *sent* is not part of a title and should not be capitalized. Choice C is incorrect.

Choice D says that *postcard* should be capitalized. *Postcard* is a common noun. In this sentence, it is not part of a name, title, or other proper noun. *Postcard* does not need to be capitalized in this sentence, so D is incorrect.

PRONOUNS

Pronouns are words that are used to stand in for nouns. There are several different types of pronouns, but the two main types are subjective and objective pronouns. **Subjective** nouns and pronouns that those that are the subject of a sentence. **Objective** nouns and pronouns are those that are an object in a sentence. Another important type of pronoun is the personal pronoun, which refers to people. Personal pronouns can be subjective or objective. **Possessive** nouns and pronouns show possession or ownership. Pronouns can also be singular or plural.

Singular

Subjective	Objective	Possessive
I	Me	My, Mine
You	You	Your, Yours
He	Him	His
She	Her	Her, hers
It	It	Its
Who	Whom	Whose

Plural

Subjective	Objective	Possessive
we	us	our, ours
you	you	your, yours
they	them	their, theirs

Review Video: Nouns and Pronouns
Visit mometrix.com/academy and enter code: 312073

Example

Choose the best pronoun to replace *Sarah's* in the following sentence.

Sarah woke up early so she could travel to see Sarah's favorite band perform in a concert.

a. Her
b. She's
c. She
d. Hers

Choice A says that *Sarah's* should be replaced with *her*. The apostrophe and *s* in *Sarah's* show that the appropriate pronoun is possessive. This means that the correct pronoun is either *her* or *hers*. When *her* is used as a possessive pronoun, it acts like an adjective and usually comes before the object. *Hers* can also act like an adjective, but it comes after the object. *Sarah's* comes before the object, *band*. This means that *her* is the appropriate choice and A is correct.

Choice B says that *Sarah's* should be replaced with *she's*. *She's* is a contraction for *she is*. This would create the following sentence: Sarah woke up early so she could travel to see she is favorite band perform in a concert. This sentence does not make sense, so B is incorrect.

Choice C says that *Sarah's* should be replaced with *she*. *She* is a subjective pronoun. *Sarah* is the subject, but the word that needs to be replaced is *Sarah's*. *Sarah's* is possessive, so it needs a possessive pronoun. This means that choice C is incorrect.

Choice D says that *Sarah's* should be replaced with *hers*. *Hers* is a possessive pronoun, but it is usually used after the object. The object in the sentence is *band*, so *Sarah's* comes before the object. Choice D is incorrect.

EXAMPLE

Which pronoun should go in the blank?

She gave her old rug to Thelma and ___.

a. I
b. We
c. Me
d. Our

In this sentence, there is a missing word. A good place to start when answering this question is to consider which part of the sentence is missing a word. Since this sentence only has one clause, a good place to start is with the subject, verb, and object. What is the verb? *Gave* is the verb, so the subject must be *she*, since she gave the old rug. This leaves the object. However, it looks like this sentence has a direct and indirect object. What is being given? Her old rug is being given, so it is the direct object. This means that the missing word is part of the indirect object.

The question says that the missing word is a pronoun. Not only is it a pronoun, but it must be an objective pronoun because it is part of the indirect object.

Choice A forms this sentence: She gave her old rug to Thelma and I. *I* is a subjective pronoun, meaning it should only be used in the subject of the sentence. The missing word must be an objective pronoun, so A is incorrect.

Choice B forms this sentence: She gave her old rug to Thelma and we. *We* is a plural and subjective pronoun. While the missing word could be singular or plural, it must be objective, so B is incorrect.

Choice C forms this sentence: She gave her old rug to Thelma and me. *Me* is an objective pronoun that completes the sentence. C is correct!

Choice D forms this sentence: She gave her old rug to Thelma and our. *Our* is a possessive pronoun. Since it also acts as an adjective, *our* also must be followed by a noun, so it cannot be the missing word. D is incorrect.

VERBS

If you want to write a sentence, then you need a verb. Without a verb, you have no sentence. The verb of a sentence indicates action or being. In other words, the verb shows something's action or state of being or the action that has been done to something.

ACTION VERBS AND LINKING VERBS

Action verbs show what the subject is doing. In other words, an action verb shows action. **Linking verbs** link the subject of a sentence to a noun or pronoun. They can also link a subject to an adjective, so the linking verb helps create a description. You always need a verb if you want a complete sentence. However, linking verbs on their own cannot be a complete sentence. Any verb that shows a condition and connects to a noun, pronoun, or adjective that describes the subject of a sentence is a linking verb.

Action: He sings. | Run! | Go! | I talk with him every day. | She reads.

Linking:

Incorrect: I am.

Correct: I am John. | The roses smell lovely. | I feel tired.

Review Video: Action Verbs and Linking Verbs
Visit mometrix.com/academy and enter code: 743142

Verb Tenses

A verb **tense** shows the different form of a verb to point to the time of an action. The present and past tense are indicated by the verb's form. An action in the present, *I talk,* can change form for the past: *I talked*. However, for future tense, an auxiliary, or helping, verb is sometimes needed to show the change in form.

Present: I talk
Past: I talked
Future: I will talk

Present: The action happens at the current time.

Example: He *walks* to the store every morning.

Past: The action happened in the past.

Example: He *walked* to the store an hour ago.

Future: The action is going to happen later.

Example: I *will walk* to the store tomorrow.

Example

What tense is the following sentence in?

David will walk to the store in three hours.

a. Present
b. Past
c. Future
d. Linking

Choice A says that the sentence is in present tense. The verb in this sentence is *walk*, but it is paired with the helping verb *will*. *Walk* is a present-tense verb, but the helping verb puts the whole verb and the sentence in the future tense. Choice A is incorrect.

Choice B says that the sentence is in the past tense. The past-tense form of *walk* is *walked*. *Walked* is not the verb used in this sentence, so this sentence is not in past tense. Choice B is incorrect.

Choice C says that the sentence is in the future tense. The future tense of the verb *walk* is *will walk*. This is the same verb that is in the sentence, so choice C is correct.

Choice D says that the sentence is in the linking tense. Remember that there are action verbs and linking verbs. However, these are not verb tenses, so there is no such thing as a linking tense. Choice D is incorrect.

EXAMPLE

Which of the following words should go in the blank?

My mother _____ me about the big nest of ants near the sandbox. I thanked her for telling me!

a. Warn
b. Warned
c. Warnt
d. Warns

First, look at the sentences. The first sentence does not have enough information to show which tense it is in. However, the second sentence says that the child thanked the mother. The verb here is *thanked*, which is the past-tense form of *thank*. Because the second sentence is in the past tense, it makes sense to say that the first sentence is also in past tense.

Choice A says that the missing word is *warn. Warn* is a present-tense verb, but it can also be used in the future tense if a helping verb is present. However, this sentence is in past tense, so it needs a past-tense verb. Choice A is wrong.

Choice B says that the missing word is *warned. Warned* is a past-tense verb, and it logically completes the sentence. Choice B is correct!

Choice C says that the missing word is *warnt.* Most verbs are regular verbs, which means that when they are in their past-tense form, the suffix *-ed* is added to the verb. When irregular verbs are in their past-tense form, they may be spelled differently. Since *warn* is a regular verb, its past-tense form is *warned. Warnt* is not the past-tense form of *warn*, and it is not a real word. Choice C is incorrect.

Choice D says that the missing word is *warns. Warn* is usually used with plural subjects, and *warns* is used with single subjects. *Warns* can be used in the future or present tense, but it cannot be used in the past tense. Since the sentence is in the past tense, it needs a past-tense verb, so D is incorrect.

ADJECTIVES

An **adjective** is a word that is used to modify a noun or pronoun. An adjective answers a question: *Which one? What kind?* or *How many?* Usually, adjectives come before the words that they modify, but they may also come after a linking verb.

Which one? The *third* suit is my favorite.

What kind? This suit is *navy blue.*

How many? I am going to buy *four* pairs of socks to match the suit.

COMPARISON WITH ADJECTIVES

Some adjectives are relative, and other adjectives are absolute. Adjectives that are **relative** can show the comparison between things. **Absolute** adjectives can also show comparison, but they do so in a different way. Let's say that you are reading two books. You think that one book is perfect, and the other book is not exactly perfect. It is not possible for one book to be more perfect than the other. Either you think that the book is perfect, or you think that the book is imperfect. In this case, perfect and imperfect are absolute adjectives.

Relative adjectives will show the different **degrees** of something or someone to something else or someone else. The three degrees of adjectives include positive, comparative, and superlative.

The **positive** degree is the normal form of an adjective.

Example: This work is *difficult.* | She is *smart.*

The **comparative** degree compares one person or thing to another person or thing.

Example: This work is *more difficult* than your work. | She is *smarter* than me.

The **superlative** degree compares more than two people or things.

Example: This is the *most difficult* work of my life. | She is the *smartest* lady in school.

Review Video: Adjectives
Visit mometrix.com/academy and enter code: 470154

EXAMPLE

What type of adjective is used in the following sentence?

The day John got married was the happiest day of his life.

a. Absolute
b. Comparative
c. Positive
d. Superlative

First find the adjective. The noun that is being described is *day*, so the adjective is *happiest.* Remember the difference between the different types of adjectives. Can one day be happier than another? How many days are being compared?

Choice A says *happiest* is an absolute adjective. Absolute adjectives cannot have different degrees. This sentence says that it was the happiest day of John's life, which means that it was happier than other days in his life. This means that *happiest* cannot be an absolute adjective, so A is incorrect.

Choice B says *happiest* is a comparative adjective. Comparative adjectives are used to compare two nouns. If John's wedding day is the happiest day of his life, then that day is being compared to thousands of other days. Also, *happiest* has the suffix *-est*, which is used in superlative adjectives that compare more than two nouns. These two facts show that *happiest* is not a comparative noun, so B is incorrect.

Choice C says that *happiest* is a positive adjective. Positive adjectives are the types of adjectives that simply describe nouns, but can be changed to either the comparative or superlative form. *Happy* is a positive noun because it can be used to describe a noun, but it can also be changed to *happier* or *happiest* in order to compare things. Since *happy* is a positive adjective that can be changed to *happiest* when more than two happy things are being compared, *happiest* is not a positive adjective. C is incorrect.

Choice D says that *happiest* is a superlative adjective. Superlative adjectives are used to compare three or more nouns. Since each of the thousands of days in John's life are being compared, it is true that more than three nouns are being compared. Again, the suffix *-est* is also used, which shows that this adjective is superlative. D is correct!

EXAMPLE

Choose the word, or words, that best completes the sentence.

Marie's meeting was ____ than Dana's meeting.

a. The most boring
b. More boring
c. Boring
d. Bored

Choice A says that *the most boring* best completes the sentence. In the sentence, one meeting is being compared to another, so only two meetings are being compared. Since choice A uses the word *most,* this choice is a superlative adjective. Superlative adjectives are used to compare three or more nouns, not two. Choice A is incorrect.

Choice B says that *more boring* best completes the sentence. This choice uses the word *more,* instead of *most. More* is used in comparative adjectives to compare two nouns. Since two meetings are being compared in the sentence, the comparative adjective *more boring* is the best choice. B is correct.

Choice C says that *boring* best completes the sentence. The only word in this answer choice is *boring,* which is a positive adjective used to describe a noun. While the sentence suggests that both meetings were boring, the sentence is comparing the two meetings. Positive adjectives are used to describe, not compare, so choice C is incorrect.

Choice D says that *bored* best completes the sentence. Like choice C, *bored* is a positive adjective used to describe a noun. Since positive adjectives without words like *more* or *most* or suffixes like *-er* or *-est* are not used to compare, *bored* is not a good choice for this sentence. *Bored* is also used to describe a state or emotion, so it is not logical to describe a meeting as bored in this sentence. D is incorrect.

ADVERBS

An **adverb** is a word that is used to **modify,** or describe, a verb, adjective, or another adverb. Usually, adverbs answer one of these questions: *When? Where? How?* and *Why?* The negatives *not* and *never* are considered adverbs. Adverbs that modify adjectives or other adverbs **strengthen** or **weaken** the words that they modify.

Examples:

He walks *quickly* through the crowd.

The water flows *smoothly* on the rocks.

Note: Adverbs are usually indicated by the suffix *-ly,* which has been added to the root word. For instance, *quick* can be made into an adverb by adding *-ly* to construct *quickly.* Some words that end in *-ly* do not follow this rule and can function as other parts of speech. Examples of adjectives ending in *-ly* include: *early, friendly, holy, lonely, silly,* and *ugly.* To know if a word that ends in *-ly* is an adjective or adverb, check your dictionary. Also, while many adverbs end in *-ly,* you need to remember that not all adverbs end in *-ly.*

Examples:

He is *never* angry.

You are *too* irresponsible to travel alone.

Types of Adverbs

Different types of adverbs are used to describe particular aspects of a verb, adjective, or other adverb. The following are examples of common types of adverbs:

Time: Some adverbs show when something was done, such as *yesterday*, *today*, or *in two days*.

Manner: Some adverbs show the way something was done, such as *hurriedly*, *neatly*, *grumpily*, or *loudly*.

Frequency: Some adverbs show how often something was done, such as *seldom*, *often*, *never*, or *often*.

Comparison with Adverbs

The rules for comparing adverbs are the same as the rules for adjectives.

The **positive** degree is the standard form of an adverb.

Example: He arrives *soon*. | She speaks *softly* to her friends.

The **comparative** degree compares one person or thing to another person or thing.

Example: He arrives *sooner* than Sarah. | She speaks *more softly* than him.

The **superlative** degree compares more than two people or things.

Example: He arrives *soonest* of the group. | She speaks the *most softly* of any of her friends.

Review Video: Adverbs
Visit mometrix.com/academy and enter code: 713951

Example

Identify the adverb in the following sentence.

I will finish both of my projects next week.

a. Will
b. My projects
c. Next week
d. Both

This example says to find the adverb in the sentence. Remember that adverbs modify, or describe, verbs or other adverbs. Adverbs are a part of speech. When looking at the answer choices, it is helpful to think about which part of speech each answer choice belongs to.

Choice A, *will*, is a verb in this sentence. While *will* comes before another verb in this sentence, *finish*, it does not describe the verb. Choice A is incorrect.

Choice B is *my projects*. These words are part of the object of the sentence, and the verbs give information about them. However, neither word is an adverb, so choice B is incorrect.

Choice C is *next week*. In the sentence, *next week* describes when the speaker will finish the projects. This means that *next week* describes the verb in the sentence by showing when the verb will be done. This makes *next week* an adverb that shows time. Choice C is correct.

Choice D is *both*. In this sentence, *both* tells how many projects the speaker has to finish. *Both* does not modify a verb, so D is incorrect.

PREPOSITIONS

A **preposition** is a word placed before a noun or pronoun that shows the relationship between an object and another word in the sentence.

Common prepositions:

about	before	during	on	under
after	beneath	for	over	until
against	between	from	past	up
among	beyond	in	through	with
around	by	of	to	within
at	down	off	toward	without

Examples:

The napkin is *in* the drawer.

The Earth rotates *around* the Sun.

The needle is *beneath* the haystack.

Can you find "me" *among* the words?

PREPOSITIONAL PHRASES

One important thing to know about prepositions is that they form special phrases, called prepositional phrases. A **prepositional phrase** begins with a preposition and ends with a noun or pronoun that is the object of the preposition. Normally, the prepositional phrase functions as an **adjective** or an **adverb** within the sentence.

Examples:

The picnic is [on the blanket] (prepositional phrase: on the blanket)

I am sick with a fever today. (prepositional phrase: with a fever)

Among the many flowers, John found a four-leaf clover. (prepositional phrase: Among the many flowers)

Review Video: Prepositions
Visit mometrix.com/academy and enter code: 946763

EXAMPLE

Which of the following could NOT complete the sentence?

She went ____ the cave.

a. Sadly
b. Into
c. From
d. Through

Choice A says that the missing word is *sadly*. The blank is between *went* and *the cave*, meaning that the missing word will connect these pieces of the sentence. While *sadly* could be used here to show how the girl felt, there would still be missing information. A preposition is needed here to show whether she entered, exited, or stood outside of the cave. *Sadly* is an adverb, so A is the correct answer.

Choice B says that *into* would complete the sentence. Does *into* complete the sentence without leaving missing information? To say *she went into the cave* is a logical, complete sentence. Choice B is incorrect.

Choice C says that the missing word is *from*. This creates the sentence *she went from the cave*. Since she could have left the cave to go somewhere else, this is also a logical, complete sentence. Choice C is incorrect.

Choice D says that *through* would complete the sentence. The sentence would read *she went through the cave*. Since she could have explored the whole cave or found an exit on the other side of it, *through* can logically complete the sentence. Choice D is incorrect.

EXAMPLE

Identify the prepositional phrase in the following sentence.

Mable visited the store to buy some vegetables.

a. To buy
b. Visited the store
c. The store to buy
d. To buy some vegetables

Remember the pieces of a prepositional phrase. Prepositional phrases should begin with a preposition and end with a noun or pronoun. Considering these rules, can any of the answer choices be eliminated? Choice B and choice C can be eliminated because neither choice begins with a preposition!

That leaves choices A and D. Choice A says that the prepositional phrase is *to buy*. This does start with a preposition, and it does give more information about Mable's trip to the store. However, it does not end with a noun or pronoun. Choice D says that the prepositional phrase is *to buy some vegetables*. Choice D begins with a preposition and ends with a noun, and it explains why Mabel went to the store.

Choice D is the only choice that has all of the pieces of a prepositional phrase, so D is correct!

CONJUNCTIONS

Conjunctions join words, phrases, or clauses and they show the connection between the joined pieces. **Coordinating conjunctions** connect equal parts of sentences. Coordinating conjunctions can also be used to create compound subjects and compound predicates, in addition to compound sentences. The **coordinating conjunctions** include *and, but, yet, or, nor, for,* and *so.*

Compound Subjects:

compound subject: Terry *and* Marissa

Terry *and* Marissa went to the movies last Saturday.

compund subject: pumpkin pie *or* apple pie

Either pumpkin pie *or* apple pie would be a good dessert to bring to Thanksgiving dinner.

compound subject: the clownfish *nor* the goldfish

Neither the clownfish *nor* the goldfish liked the new fish food very much.

Compound Predicates:

compound predicate: left school *and* picked up her sister

Veronica left school *and* picked up her sister from soccer practice.

compound predicate: take a nap *or* play with the dog

The cat did not take a nap *or* play with the dog yesterday.

Compound Sentences:

The rock was small, *but* it was heavy.

She drove in the night, *and* he drove in the day.

Bill dressed nicely today, *for* he must give an important presentation this afternoon.

EXAMPLE

Read the sentence below and answer the following question.

Joseph went grocery shopping and put all of the groceries away when he got home.

In the sentence, the conjunction and helps create a compound...

a. Sentence
b. Subject
c. Predicate
d. Clause

In the sentence, where does the word *and* appear? Is it between two subjects, two verbs, or two independent clauses?

Find the subject of the sentence. Who did the actions in the sentence? Joseph did. While both *Joseph* and *he* are subjects in this sentence, they are not joined by *and* in this sentence, so the sentence does not contain a compound subject. Additionally, *Joseph* is the subject of an independent clause, while *he* is the subject of a dependent clause. Since this sentence contains a dependent clause, it is not a compound sentence. Choices A and B are incorrect.

Since *and* does not join two subjects or independent clauses, consider the verbs in the sentence, *went* and *put*. *And* is used in the sentence to show that Joseph did two actions. This information makes up the predicate, so the word *and* does help create a compound predicate. Choice C is correct.

While conjunctions can join clauses to form compound sentences, there is no such thing as a compound clause. Choice D is incorrect.

End Punctuation

Periods

Use a period to end all sentences except direct questions and exclamations. Periods are also used for abbreviations.

Examples: 3 p.m. | 2 a.m. | Mr. Jones | Mrs. Stevens | Dr. Smith | Bill, Jr. | Pennsylvania Ave.

Note: An abbreviation is a shortened form of a word or phrase.

Question Marks

Question marks should be used following a **direct question**. A polite request can be followed by a period instead of a question mark.

Direct Question: What is for lunch today? | How are you? | Why is that the answer?

Polite Requests: Can you please send me the item tomorrow. | Will you please walk with me on the track.

Review Video: Question Marks
Visit mometrix.com/academy and enter code: 118471

Exclamation Marks

Exclamation marks are used after a word group or sentence that shows much feeling or has special importance. Exclamation marks should not be overused. They are saved for proper **exclamatory interjections**.

Example: We're going to the finals! | You have a beautiful car! | "That's crazy!" she yelled.

Review Video: Exclamation Points
Visit mometrix.com/academy and enter code: 199367

Commas

The comma is a punctuation mark that can help you understand connections in a sentence. Not every sentence needs a comma. However, if a sentence needs a comma, you need to put it in the right place. A comma in the wrong place or a missing comma will make a sentence's meaning unclear. These are some of the rules for commas:

Use Case	Example
Before a **coordinating conjunction** joining independent clauses in compound sentences	Bob caught three fish, and I caught two fish.
Between **items in a series**	I will bring the turkey, the pie, and the coffee.
After **transition words**	Consequently, Joel's mother grounded him.

Review Video: When To Use a Comma
Visit mometrix.com/academy and enter code: 786797

EXAMPLE

Choose the correct location for a comma in the following sentence.

Emily's dad reminded her five times to put her plate away but she still forgot.

a. After *away*
b. After *times*
c. After *but*
d. After *dad*

Remember that there are specific reasons for using commas in sentences. Are there any pieces of this sentence that look like they should be separated by a comma? There are not any lists, prepositional phrases, or transitions in this sentence. There are also not any phrases or dependent clauses. However, there are two independent clauses. Remember that independent clauses can be joined by conjunctions, and when they are joined by coordinating conjunctions, a comma is needed.

Look at the sentence and first identify the independent clauses. The sentence starts by saying that Emily's dad has reminded her to put her plate away. There is a subject, Emily's dad, and a predicate that gives information about his actions. Later in the sentence, Emily does an action, so she is the subject. This means that the first independent clause must be the information about Emily's dad. This clause ends just before the word *but* because Emily then becomes the subject. This means that *but* is the conjunction. Since it is a coordinating conjunction, this is a compound sentence.

Now consider the answer choices. Choices B and D can both be eliminated because they are not near the conjunction. This leaves A, after *away*, and C, after *but*. Commas are used just before coordinating conjunctions in compound sentences, so choice A is correct.

EXAMPLE

Which of the following words in the sentence should NOT be followed by a comma?

My mother gave me my sister my dad and my brother four presents each.

a. Sister
b. Me
c. Dad
d. Brother

Like in the previous example, a good first step for answering this question is to identify why a comma is needed. Look at the pieces of the sentence, such as the subject, predicate, and any objects or verbs. There are three objects in a row in this sentence. This looks like a list! Remember that in lists, commas go after each item except for the last one. The sentence should look like this: My mother gave me, my sister, my dad, and my brother four presents each. There is a comma after *me*, *sister*, and *dad*. This eliminates choices A, C, and B. Choice D is the correct answer, since there is no reason that *brother* should be followed by a comma in this sentence.

APOSTROPHES

An apostrophe is used to show **possession** or the **deletion of letters in contractions**. An apostrophe is not needed with the possessive pronouns *his, hers, its, ours, theirs, whose*, and *yours*.

APOSTROPHES SHOWING POSSESSION

Singular Nouns: David's car | a book's theme | my brother's board game

Plural Nouns that end with -*s*: the scissors' handle | boys' basketball

Plural Nouns that end without -*s*: Men's department | the people's adventure

APOSTROPHES IN CONTRACTIONS

Contractions are combinations of words. Contractions involve taking two words, removing at least one letter from one of the words, putting an apostrophe in its place, and removing the space. For example, *does not* can be written as the contraction *doesn't*. The *o* is removed from *not* and is replaced with an apostrophe, which represents the removed letter, so it appears as *n't*. The space after does is then removed, turning *does not* into the contraction *doesn't*. Not all words can be used to form contractions, but many small, commonly used words can. More examples of contractions are listed below.

First Word	Second Word	Contraction
Can	Not	Can't
Do	Not	Don't
She	Will	She'll
They	Will	They'll
He	Is	He's
It	Is	It's
They	Are	They're
I	Am	I'm

Review Video: When to Use an Apostrophe
Visit mometrix.com/academy and enter code: 213068

Review Video: Punctuation Errors in Possessive Pronouns
Visit mometrix.com/academy and enter code: 221438

EXAMPLE

Choose the correct possessive form of family in this sentence.

My familys Christmas card looks great this year!

a. Families'
b. Family's
c. Familys'
d. The word is already spelled correctly.

Before thinking about each choice, look closely at the sentence. The instructions say that the answer should be possessive. Since *family* is not a pronoun, the answer must have an apostrophe. Where should the apostrophe go? Recall the rules about apostrophes for singular nouns, plural nouns, and plural nouns ending in *s*.

Choice A says the correct spelling is *families'*. This word ends in *-ies*. Remember that when singular nouns ending in *y* are changed to the plural form, they are usually changed to end in *-ies*. Also, when plural possessive nouns end in *s*, the apostrophe goes after the *s*, and there is not another *s* added after it. Choice A is the correct plural possessive form of *family*. However, this is not the correct answer because the sentence is only talking about one family. A is incorrect.

Choice B says the correct spelling is *family's*. This is the singular possessive form of *family*. Unlike the sentence in the instructions, this choice has an apostrophe after the *y* in *familys*. The sentence is talking about the Christmas card belonging to one family, so this is the correct form. Choice B is correct.

Choice C says the correct spelling is *familys'*. This choice is not the correct singular possessive form or the correct plural possessive form of *family*. Choice C is incorrect.

Choice D says that *familys* is correct. This choice does not have an apostrophe. Remember that an apostrophe is needed for all possessive nouns and is only left out of possessive pronouns. Since *family* is not a pronoun, choice D is incorrect.

EXAMPLE

Choose the correct contraction form of should not.

a. Shou'dnt
b. Should'nt
c. Shouldn'ot
d. Shouldn't

Remember what contractions are and how they are formed. Two words are combined into one by using an apostrophe in the place of a letter. Sometimes the remaining letters are changed. The apostrophe must fill the space left by the letter that was removed.

Choice A says that the contraction formed by *should* and *not* is *shou'dnt*. In this choice, the *l* in *should* and the *o* in *not* have been removed. Only one of these letters, *l*, has been replaced by an apostrophe. This is not a proper contraction, since any missing letter should be replaced with an apostrophe. Choice A is incorrect.

Choice B says that the contraction formed by *should* and *not* is *should'nt*. In this choice, the *o* in *not* is missing and there is an apostrophe between *d* and *n*. The apostrophe is in the wrong place, since it should be used in place of the *o* to show that *o* is missing. Choice B is incorrect.

Choice C says that the contraction formed by *should* and *not* is *shouldn'ot*. In this choice, no letters have been removed, but an apostrophe has been added between *n* and *o* in *not*. This contraction is not written correctly because no letters have been removed. Choice C is incorrect.

Choice D says that the contraction formed by *should* and *not* is *shouldn't*. In this choice, the o in not has been removed and replaced with an apostrophe. There is only one missing letter and one apostrophe, and the apostrophe has been placed where the missing letter originally was. This contraction is written correctly, so choice D is correct.

CAPITALIZATION

One important part of using correct grammar is properly capitalizing words. Usually, only nouns will be capitalized, but there are some exceptions. The most important capitalization rule is that the first word of every sentence, no matter what part of speech it is, should be capitalized. Another exception is that the pronoun *I* should always be capitalized.

Proper nouns are always capitalized, but sometimes it can be tricky to decide whether or not a noun is a proper noun. Some words that are usually common nouns may become proper nouns when used with other words or phrases. Also, when words that are not nouns are used with a noun, or when a group of words are used together as one noun, those words may also need to be capitalized.

TITLES OF PEOPLE

A title is a word that goes with a person's name and gives others information about them. These words are usually common nouns that are not capitalized alone, but when they are used with a person's name, they are capitalized. For example, the word *president* is not a proper noun, so it is not always capitalized. However, it should be capitalized when it is used with a person's name or in place of a person's name. For example, in the phrase *President George Washington*, the title is part of a person's name.

HOLIDAYS

Names of specific holidays should be capitalized. Holidays that are more general or, like birthdays and anniversaries, should not be capitalized. Words that can go with the names of specific holidays, like *day*, should also be capitalized when used in the name of a holiday.

Example:

> My brother's birthday is the day after Christmas Day.

GEOGRAPHIC NAMES

Names of specific places, areas, and regions are proper nouns, so they should always be capitalized. The cardinal directions, north, south, east, and west, should be capitalized when they are part of the name of a specific place or area. However, cardinal directions should not be capitalized when used outside of the name of a place.

Review Video: Capitalization in Grammar
Visit mometrix.com/academy and enter code: 369678

Example

Choose the word that should NOT be capitalized in the sentence below.

The next Governor will be Professor Goodman because he received the most votes on Election Day.

a. Governor
b. Professor
c. Election
d. Day

Choice A says that *governor* should not be capitalized. *Governor* is a title, which means that it may or not be capitalized depending on how it is used in the sentence. While we know that Professor Goodman is the next governor, the word is still not used as part of his name in this sentence. The word *governor* is a common noun, so it should not be capitalized. Choice A is correct.

Choice B says that *professor* should not be capitalized. Remember the rules for capitalizing people's titles. If the title is used as a part of the person's name, it should be capitalized. While *professor* is not a proper noun by itself, it goes with a person's name in this sentence, creating the whole name *Professor Goodman*. Choice B is incorrect.

Choice C says that *election* should not be capitalized. The word *election* is part of the name of a national holiday. Since Election Day is a specific holiday, it is a proper noun. *Election* should be capitalized in this sentence, so C is incorrect.

Choice D says that *day* should not be capitalized. Election Day is a specific holiday and a proper noun. Remember that words that are part of the name of a holiday are also capitalized, even small words like *day*. *Day* is supposed to be capitalized in this sentence, so C is incorrect.

Chapter Quiz

1. Every sentence always has a subject and a/an:

a. Imperative
b. Preposition
c. Predicate
d. Modifier

2. Which of the following sentences does NOT have an implied subject?

a. Take John on a quick walk.
b. Don't get lost.
c. John knows the way to the park.
d. Bring me back some flowers.

3. Which pronoun can be either singular or plural depending on what it is representing in the context of the sentence?

a. Nobody
b. Either
c. Several
d. All

4. Which of the following is written in third person perspective?

a. I am walking
b. He is walking
c. You are walking
d. We are walking

5. Which of the following best describes the function of an indirect object?

a. Shows how an action had an influence
b. Takes or receives the action of a verb
c. Explains or describes the subject
d. Shows that there is more information needed

6. Which of the following is a group of words that contains both a subject and a verb, and can be either independent or dependent?

a. Antecedent
b. Fragment
c. Phrase
d. Clause

7. Which of the following is a word placed before a noun or pronoun that shows the relationship between an object and another word in the sentence?

a. Adjective
b. Adverb
c. Preposition
d. Conjunction

CHAPTER QUIZ ANSWER KEY

1. C: See section **Predicates**

2. C: See section **Subjects**

3. D: See section **Depend on Context**

4. B: See section **Person Agreement Examples**

5. A: See section **Indirect Objects**

6. D: See section **Clauses**

7. C: See section **Prepositions**

Written Essay

ESSAYS

Essays usually focus on one topic, subject, or goal. There are several types of essays, including informative, persuasive, and narrative. An essay's structure and formality depend on the type of essay and its goal. While narrative essays typically do not include outside sources, other types of essays often require some research and the use of primary and secondary sources.

The basic format of an essay typically has three major parts: the introduction, the body, and the conclusion. The body is further divided into the writer's main points. Most essays will have at least three main points, but essays that go into more depth can have almost any number of main points.

An essay's introduction should answer three questions:

1. What is the **subject** of the essay?

   If an essay is about a book, the answer would include the title and author of the book, as well as any additional information needed, such as the subject or argument of the book.

2. How does the essay **discuss** the subject?

   To answer this, the writer briefly summarizes the main points and the evidence supporting them to let readers know how the essay is organized and what information they can expect to read.

3. What will the essay **prove**?

   This information is in the thesis statement, usually the opening paragraph's last sentence, which clearly states the writer's message.

The body elaborates on all the main points related to the thesis, introducing one main point at a time, and includes supporting evidence with each main point. Each body paragraph should state the point in a topic sentence, which is usually the first sentence in the paragraph. The paragraph should then explain the point's meaning, support it with quotations or other evidence, and then explain how this point and the evidence are related to the thesis. The writer should then repeat this procedure in a new paragraph for each additional main point.

The conclusion restates the content of the introduction, including the thesis, to remind the reader of the essay's main argument or subject. The essay writer may also summarize the highlights of the argument or description contained in the body of the essay, following the same organization originally used in the body. For example, a conclusion might look like: Point 1 + Point 2 + Point 3 = Thesis, or Point 1 → Point 2 → Point 3 → Thesis Proof. Good organization makes essays easier for writers to compose and provides a guide for readers to follow. Well-organized essays hold attention better and are more likely to get readers to believe or agree with the writer.

Using Sources in Essays

Sometimes writers use information from others in their work. This is most common in expository and persuasive writing. For an expository essay, a writer may not know all of the information that he or she needs to finish the composition. The writer may use other people's work to find the missing information and complete the composition. Persuasive writers may do research to find facts or statements from others that support their own beliefs and make their writing more persuasive. In both cases, research helps the writer find information that **supports** his or her **original work**.

Outside information must be relevant, true, and helpful to be appropriate for a composition. Writers must also be careful not to use too much outside information, since this can make the composition unoriginal. If a writer does use outside information, it is extremely important that the writer mention in the composition where the information came from. If the writer forgets or chooses not to say where the information came from, he or she has stolen someone else's work and presented it as their own. Doing this is called **plagiarism**.

Informational Texts

Informational texts, also called instructional or expository texts, are compositions written to inform the reader about a specific topic. An informational essay can inform readers in a variety of ways, such as giving them instructions, telling them facts about the topic, or teaching them why something happens. Informational texts should be logical, meaning that they should present information in an order that the reader can easily understand, and they should include the right amount of information so the writer successfully informs his or her audience of new information.

Informational texts should also focus on a **controlling idea**. In the introduction of an informational text, there may be a sentence or two that clearly state the essay's controlling idea. This sentence, or sentences, is called a **thesis statement**. The controlling idea should be clear throughout the composition. By emphasizing the controlling idea in the introduction, body, and conclusion, the writer can ensure that the controlling idea is clear. One way to make sure that the controlling idea is emphasized is to think about the purpose of each part of the essay. The introduction prepares the reader by telling them what the rest of the essay is about, so the controlling idea should be **introduced** in this section. The body tells the reader the information the writer wants to tell the audience, so this **explains** the controlling idea and facts about it to the reader. The conclusion is used to **remind** the reader of how the information in the body is related and **restates** the controlling idea one final time.

Review Video: Informational Text
Visit mometrix.com/academy and enter code: 924964

Structures or Organizational Patterns in Informational Texts

Informational text can be **descriptive**, meaning that it gives information that can be experienced through the five senses, or it answers the questions what, who, when, where, and why. One common method of organizing informational text is to put it in a certain sequence, or order. **Chronological** texts include events in the order that they occurred, from start to finish. **How-to**, or **instructional**, texts organize information into a series of instructions in the order in which the steps should be followed. **Comparison-contrast** structures of informational text describe different ideas to their readers by pointing out how things or ideas are similar and how they are different. **Cause and effect** structures of informational text describe events that occurred and the causes or reasons for those events. **Problem and solution** structures of informational texts introduce and describe problems and offer one or more solutions for each problem described.

Argumentative Writing

In argumentative writing, the writer expresses a belief or opinion that he or she wants to lead readers to agree with. When writing an argumentative composition, the writer should first identify the **topic** his or her opinion is about. The topic may be serious or fun, as long as there is one clear topic in the composition. The next step is for the writer to determine his or her opinion on the topic and determine why he or she holds that opinion. In order to persuade others to agree with their opinion, the writer must be able to give readers reasons to support the opinion. If the writer does not know why he or she has an opinion, it will be difficult to convince readers to agree. In addition to having reasons that support their opinion, writers should prepare examples that support each of these reasons in order to strengthen their composition.

Once the writer has determined his or her topic, opinion, and reasons for having the opinion, he or she is ready to begin writing an argumentative essay. In the introduction, the writer should capture the reader's interest, introduce the topic, and reveal his or her opinion about the topic. In the body of the composition, the writer should remind the reader of the opinion and give his or her reasons for holding the opinion. If the writer has any examples, facts, or other information that supports his or her opinion or reasons for believing it, these should also be included in the body. Writers may also use a body paragraph to mention opposing opinions or beliefs and explain why they disagree with them. As in other compositions, the conclusion should remind the reader of the essay's topic and purpose, as well as remind the reader how the opinion has been explained and supported. The conclusion should also invite the reader to continue thinking about the topic and writer's opinion. This can be done through questions or statements that lead readers to consider whether or not they agree with the author's opinion or what their own opinions are.

Review Video: Argumentative Writing
Visit mometrix.com/academy and enter code: 561544

Informative vs. Persuasive Writing

Informative writing, also called explanatory or expository writing, is written to show that something is true or factual, while **persuasive** writing is written to lead the reader to agree with something that may or may not be true or factual. While persuasive text is written to **persuade** readers to agree with the author's position, informative text simply **provides information** to readers. Informative writing **informs** readers about why or how something is as it is. This can include offering new information, explaining how a process works, or describing a concept for readers.

Facts and Opinions

Writers and readers must always be aware of the difference between fact and opinion. A **fact** can be tested and proven to be true. An **opinion**, on the other hand, is someone's personal thoughts or feelings. Opinions are often not changed by information. If an author writes that a newborn elephant is about five times taller than a newborn giraffe, then he or she is stating a fact. If the author writes that giraffes are more interesting than elephants, then he or she is giving an opinion because this cannot be proven to be true or false. Opinions are often supported by facts. For instance, the author might use a comparison between the way that giraffes eat and the way elephants eat as evidence of how giraffes are more interesting. An opinion supported by facts tends to be more convincing. On the other hand, when authors support their opinions with other opinions, readers should seriously think about and read the argument carefully to see whether it is logical and trustworthy.

Review Video: Distinguishing Fact and Opinion
Visit mometrix.com/academy and enter code: 870899

Responding to a Text

An essay prompt may require writers to write about a text they have read. When writing an essay like this, writers should show that they understand the text they have read. They may mention their own thoughts, ideas, and opinions in the essay. However, the main idea of the essay should be about the text mentioned in the prompt.

When planning the essay, writers should consider what the text is about and how it is written. Writers should identify the purpose, main idea, and structure of the text. For informational and persuasive texts, they should also think about the supporting details the author used in the text. All of these facts about the text will help writers understand the text well and allow the writer to create a response to the text.

Responding to Multiple Texts

Essay prompts may ask writers to write about more than one text. In this case, writers should identify the purpose, main idea, and structure of each text. They should also look at the kinds of supporting details that the author of each text uses. Once writers know these details, they should think about the differences and similarities between the texts. The main ideas of each text may oppose each other, or one may support the other. Writers will need to write about both texts in the essay, so they must understand both texts and the connection between the texts.

Chapter Quiz

1. What type of essay does NOT typically include outside sources?

a. Expository
b. Informative
c. Persuasive
d. Narrative

2. Which of the following is NOT true of informational texts?

a. Informational texts are also called instructional or expository texts
b. Informational texts should be logical
c. Informational texts should focus on a central idea
d. Informational texts can only be structured chronologically

3. In an argumentative essay, which of the following should be included in the body?

a. A reminder of the writer's opinion and his or her reasons for holding the opinion
b. Examples, facts, or other information that supports the writer's opinion
c. Opposing opinions or beliefs and explanations of why the writer disagrees with them
d. All of the above

Chapter Quiz Answer Key

1. D: See section **Essays**

2. D: See section **Structures or Organizational Patterns in Informational Texts**

3. D: See section **Argumentative Writing**

Informational Text Example

Below is a prompt for an informational text. There is also an example of an essay that addresses the prompt. There are multiple drafts of this essay to show what kinds of changes a writer may make during the writing process to improve his or her work.

Prompt:

In school, students learn about many subjects. Write about your favorite subject and explain why it is important to people's lives outside of school.

Rough Draft

Do you think math is boring? Well, think again! Solving math problems is so fun because they are like riddles made of numbers! Houses, computers, and even rocket ships would not exist without math! Math is my favorite subject and it is important.

Math is important because our houses would look very different without it. Next time you go home, look at the outside of your house. How many different shapes do you see? Before people lived in houses, they lived in shelters like caves and tents. Math helped people learn how to make buildings, so now we can live inside! People who build houses need math so that they know what shape the house should be and how big each part should be.

Computers have made our lives easier. Now, it is possible to find almost any information in seconds! Computers also make it easier for people to communicate with each other. Phones and TVs use computers, but we also need math to use them! The only person I can think of who doesn't use a phone, TV, or computer is my baby brother. Computers use very complicated math problems, so many types of math are very important for computers to work!

The third reason math is important is that it helps people invent things like rocket ships so we can visit space. Math is used to build the rockets, make the rockets fly, and help the astronauts travel through space! Rocket ships don't affect our daily lives right now, but they can help scientists continue to invent things that could change our lives in the future. Who knows, math could help us reach Mars and find a way to live there!

As you can see from these examples, math is important because it affects our daily lives and makes it possible for us to achieve new things and think of new possibilities. If you thought math was boring before, I bet you don't think it is now!

Revised Draft

Do you think math is boring? Well, think again! Solving math problems is so fun because they are like riddles made of numbers! Houses, computers, and ~~even rocket ships~~ would not exist without math! Math is my favorite subject and it is important because it helps people complete very important jobs that affect others' daily lives.

Math is important because our houses would look very different without it. Next time you go home, look at the outside of your house. How many different shapes do you see? Before people lived in houses, they lived in shelters like caves and tents. Math helped people learn how to make buildings, so now we can live inside! People who build houses need math so that they know what shape the house should be and how big each part should be.

Computers have made our lives easier. Now, it is possible to find almost any information in seconds! Computers also make it easier for people to communicate with each other. Phones and TVs use computers, but we also need math to use them! The only person I can think of who doesn't use a phone, TV, or computer is my baby brother. Computers use very complicated math problems, so many types of math are very important for computers to work!

~~The third reason math is important is that it helps people invent things like rocket ships so we can visit space. Math is used to build the rockets, make the rockets fly, and help the astronauts travel through space! Rocket ships don't affect our daily lives right now, but they can help scientists continue to invent things that could change our lives in the future. Who knows, math could help us reach Mars and find a way to live there!~~

As you can see from these examples, math is important because it affects our daily lives and makes it possible for us to achieve new things and think of ~~new possibilities~~. Math affects where we live and how we communicate and find information. If you thought math was boring before, I bet you don't think it is now!

Revised Draft Notes

Remember the purpose of the revising stage of the writing process. When revising, it is important to look at the whole composition. Do all of the paragraphs strengthen the composition? Do the introduction and conclusion help the reader understand the controlling idea and main points?

First, look at the underlined words. These are words that have been added in the revision process. In the introduction, a clause has been added to the last sentence. This clause strengthens the composition by giving more information about the essay's controlling idea. Now this sentence, the thesis, tells the reader not only what the writer's favorite subject is, but also why the writer thinks it is important to others' lives. A sentence has been added to the conclusion, as well. This sentence strengthens the conclusion by emphasizing why the writer thinks math is important. The sentence makes the conclusion more interesting and reminds the reader of the writer's main points.

Next, look at what has been crossed out in this essay. Some words in the introduction and conclusion have been removed, and a whole paragraph has been omitted! Why is that? There were no huge errors, and the writing made sense, but those details and facts did not support the controlling idea very well. When the writer added to the introduction, he or she made the controlling idea clearer. However, the controlling idea says that math is important because it affects people's daily lives. While rocket science is important, it is not important for daily life. The writer made a smart choice to remove this information and should later replace it with more relevant information about how math impacts daily life.

EDITED DRAFT

Do you think math is boring? Well, think again! ~~Solving math problems is so fun because they are like riddles made of numbers!~~ Houses, computers, and ~~even rocket ships~~ would not exist without math! Math is my favorite subject and it is important.

Math is important because our houses would look very different without it. Next time you go home, look at the outside of your house. How many different shapes do you see? People who build houses need math so that they know what shape the house should be and how big each part should be. Before people lived in houses, they lived in shelters like caves and tents. Math helped people learn how to make buildings, so now we can live inside!

Another reason math is important is because it makes inventions like computers possible. Computers have made our lives easier. Now, it is possible to find almost any information in seconds! Computers also make it easier for people to communicate with each other. For example, devices like phones and TVs use computers, but we also need math to use them! ~~The only person I can think of who doesn't use a phone, TV, or computer is my baby brother.~~ Computers use very complicated math problems, so many types of math are very important for computers to work!

~~The third reason math is important is that it helps people invent things like rocket ships so we can visit space. Math is used to build the rockets, make the rockets fly, and help the astronauts travel through space! Rocket ships don't affect our daily lives right now, but they can help scientists continue to invent things that could change our lives in the future. Who knows, math could help us reach Mars and find a way to live there!~~

As you can see from these examples, math is important because it affects our daily lives and makes it possible for us to achieve new things and think of ~~new possibilities~~. If you thought math was boring before, I bet you don't think it is now!

Edited Draft Notes

Since the writer has revised his or her work, the next step is to edit the composition. Remember that editing is very similar to revising, but editing usually includes paying attention to each paragraph, instead of the whole composition. Look at the changes that were made to each paragraph.

In the introduction, the second sentence was removed. Why was it removed? It was a good sentence, and it gave information about math! While it was engaging and it mentioned math, it was still off topic. The prompt asks why math is important for people's lives. This sentence tells why math is enjoyable to learn about, so it does not prepare the reader for the information in the rest of the essay. Also, the introduction already has a hook, so this sentence does not help the paragraph or the composition.

What has been changed in the second paragraph? The underlined sentence was in the rough draft, but it was in a different part of the paragraph. This paragraph is about how math has affected the buildings people live in. In the rough draft, the underlined sentence was at the end! This sentence supports the paragraph, but it was not very helpful or logical at the end of the paragraph. The writer moved it in the editing step of the writing process. Now this paragraph makes more sense and its sentences are in a logical order that helps the reader understand the writer's point.

There are a few changes in the second paragraph. A sentence was added to the beginning of the paragraph. Before, the paragraph simply started by explaining that computers are convenient inventions. The new sentence is helpful because it creates a transition and tells the reader what the main point of the paragraph is. The next difference is the added words at the beginning of the fourth paragraph. These words also form a transition, and they show the reader that the sentence contains examples that support the main point of the paragraph. Finally, a sentence has been removed from this paragraph. This sentence may be related to the information in the paragraph, but it does not strengthen it or support the main point.

The remaining marks are left to remind the writer that the information about rockets and math still need to be replaced. This information will be added before the final draft is finished.

Final Draft

Do you think math is boring? Well, think again! Houses, computers, and even cars would not exist without math! Math is my favorite subject, and it is important because it helps people complete very important jobs that affect others' daily lives.

Math is important because our houses would look very different without it. Next time you go home, look at the outside of your house. How many different shapes do you see? People who build houses need math so that they know what shape the house should be and how big each part should be. Before people lived in houses, they lived in shelters like caves and tents. Math helped people learn how to make buildings, so now we can live inside!

Another reason math is important is because it makes inventions like computers possible. Computers have made our lives easier. Now, it is possible to find almost any information in seconds! Computers also make it easier for people to communicate with each other. For example, devices like phones and TVs use computers, so we also need math to use them! Computers use very complicated math problems, so many types of math are very important for computers to work!

The third reason math is important is that it helps people invent things like cars so we can travel fast. Math is used to build cars and make them drive. Cars are very important because they help us go places quickly when we are in a hurry or have an emergency. Before cars, people used wagons, horses, and trains to get around. Can you imagine how long it would take to go on vacation if you had to ride a horse? Cars are helpful and convenient, and we would not have them without math!

As you can see from these examples, math is important because it affects our daily lives and makes it possible for us to achieve new things. Math affects where we live, how we communicate and find information, and how we travel. If you thought math was boring before, I bet you don't think it is now!

Final Draft Notes

This is the final draft! In this draft, information has been added to the introduction and conclusion, and there is a new paragraph. Notice that these additions have replaced all of the information about rockets that was removed in the revising step. Now, the essay discusses how math has helped people create houses, computers, and cars. Cars impact more people's daily lives than rockets do, so these additions help strengthen the composition by supporting the controlling idea, or thesis. The additions in the introduction and conclusion make it easier for the reader to understand the writer's main points and read the composition.

Evaluation

The essay answers the prompt and is on topic throughout the composition. The controlling idea is clear and is stated in the introduction, supported in the body, and restated in the conclusion. The thesis statement restates parts of the prompt and gives the reader a preview of the rest of the essay. The body uses well-structured paragraphs to explain the supporting details and examples and connects them to the controlling idea. The conclusion also emphasizes the controlling idea and supporting details and invites the reader to consider what they have read.

The essay is also interesting and written with a variety of sentence types. It uses transitions and good paragraph structure to make the essay easy for the reader to understand. The introduction also uses a hook to get the reader's attention and help him or her relate to the information in the essay. The examples are all things that most readers will be able to see in their own lives. Not only does this essay answer the prompt and have appropriate structure, but it also makes use of good, engaging, and relatable details.

Practice Test #1

Reading

One Giant Leap for Mankind

(1) On July 20, 1969, Neil Armstrong became the first man to walk on the moon, as 500 million people around the world watched on television. This was truly a historic event. Almost all people throughout history would have laughed at the idea that, one day, a man would walk on the moon. They would have said it was impossible. They would have called a person "crazy" for even talking about the idea. But, on July 20, 1969, a man from a small Ohio town proved them wrong.

Armstrong's Childhood

(2) Neil Armstrong was born on August 5, 1930, in Wapakoneta, Ohio. His father had to travel for his job, so the Armstrong family moved about 20 times while Neil was a boy. They moved back to Wapakoneta permanently when he was 14. By this time, Neil was in love with flying. Airplanes were still new back then, and most people had never been in one, but Neil took his first plane ride when he was only six years old. He fell in love with flying, and when he was a teenager, he started taking flying lessons. He even got a license to fly before he was old enough to get a driver's license! He was also active in Boy Scouts and earned its highest rank of Eagle Scout.

Armstrong's Early Career

(3) Neil went off to college at Purdue University in Indiana right after he turned 17. He studied for two years and then served in the Navy, where he became a fighter pilot. After fighting in the Korean War, he came back to finish his college degree. After college, he joined the Air Force and became a pilot who tested new kinds of aircraft. During his career, he flew in over 200 different kinds of vehicles. It was during this time that the government created NASA to explore space, and, in 1962, Neil Armstrong was selected to train as an astronaut.

First Man on the Moon

(4) In 1961, President John F. Kennedy announced that he wanted NASA to land on the moon before 1970. That meant Neil Armstrong and the other astronauts had to work hard to get ready. The work was very dangerous, and some men died while exploring space. Neil Armstrong and the other astronauts bravely continued, though, and Neil was selected to be the first human being to set foot on the moon. After they returned to Earth, he and the other astronauts became national heroes.

Armstrong's Later Life

(5) Neil Armstrong could have used his fame to make a lot of money or run for president. Instead, he chose to live a quiet life out of the spotlight and became a college professor. He didn't go on TV or give interviews very often, and he didn't like traveling around giving speeches. He died on August 25, 2012, at age 82. Many people lead remarkable lives, but Neil Armstrong's life was truly "out of this world."

Refer to the passage "One Giant Leap for Mankind" to answer questions 1-7.

1. Which phrase below means the same thing as *permanently* in paragraph 2?

a. On time
b. Before dark
c. For good
d. At the same time

2. Notice that the passage has four sections, titled "Armstrong's Childhood," "Armstrong's Early Career," "First Man on the Moon," and "Armstrong's Later Life." Which of the following pieces of information would be found in the "First Man on the Moon" section?

a. Where Neil Armstrong attended high school
b. How old Neil Armstrong was when he got married
c. What year Neil Armstrong walked on the moon
d. How many siblings Neil Armstrong had

3. How is this passage organized?

a. It describes the history of NASA up until Neil Armstrong walked on the moon.
b. It tells how Neil Armstrong's favorite teacher inspired him to become an astronaut.
c. It explains how Neil Armstrong figured out how to fly a spaceship to the moon.
d. It shows how the events in Neil Armstrong's life led to him being the first man to walk on the moon.

4. What do the section titles "Armstrong's Childhood," "Armstrong's Early Career," "First Man on the Moon," and "Armstrong's Later Life" tell the reader?

a. Where Neil Armstrong lived during the events described in each section
b. Which part of Neil Armstrong's life each section is about
c. Where Neil Armstrong worked during the events described in each section
d. Which of Neil Armstrong's missions each section is about

5. Which of these definitions matches the way degree is used in paragraph 3?

Degree *(noun)* pronounced: dih-gree 1. the unit for a measurement of heat 2. how much of a certain quality something has 3. a confirmation that someone has graduated from college 4. the measurement of an angle

a. Definition 1
b. Definition 2
c. Definition 3
d. Definition 4

6. What is the main idea of paragraph 5?

a. Neil Armstrong chose to live a humble life after his time as an astronaut.
b. Neil Armstrong was shy person, so he avoided interviews and public appearances.
c. Neil Armstrong did not know enough about politics to run for president.
d. Neil Armstrong was not a successful astronaut, so he was not very famous.

7. Which of the following conclusions is supported by this passage?

a. All astronauts have a college degree and a pilot's license.
b. Neil Armstrong will be remembered as a historical figure.
c. All astronauts since Neil Armstrong have walked on the moon.
d. Neil Armstrong and President Kennedy became good friends.

Miguel's World

(1) Miguel Gonzalez and his father took many walks in the woods near their house. When Miguel was very young, around five, he liked to pick up branches and hit them against the ground and the trees. Sometimes he would waive the stick and pretend he was fighting a great battle. Mr. Gonzalez always told Miguel to drop the stick.

(2) "You will poke an eye out," said Mr. Gonzalez.

(3) A few years later, Miguel stopped hitting things with sticks and started asking his father about the trees and the other things he saw in the woods. Miguel's father taught him how to identify different trees by the texture of their bark and the size and shape of their leaves. Miguel found out how trees spread their seeds and what kinds of animals eat the leaves, bark, and seeds.

(4) Miguel loved taking walks with his father, but he did not appreciate all the things that he saw in the woods. One day, they almost tripped over a log that had fallen on the trail. Miguel kicked it.

(5) "Stupid log, it almost made me fall," he said.

(6) Miguel's father waved his arms, shook his head, and told his son to stop. "That's not just a piece of wood, Miguel," said Mr. Gonzalez. "That log is a home for many creatures and plants. Kicking that log would be like an earthquake to them! How would you like it if a giant ant kicked our house?"

(7) "There are ants in there?" asked Miguel.

(8) "Watch," said Mr. Gonzalez. He brushed the old, brown leaves and rotting bark off the top of the log until they could see the wood buried underneath. On the smooth surface were clusters of small, dark holes. An ant poked its head from one of the holes.

(9) Miguel laughed. "Is there anything else in that log?" Miguel asked.

(10) "Let's see," said Mr. Gonzalez. The two brushed off more leaves. They worked carefully to avoid touching the slimy slugs that dotted the log. Near the end of the rotten piece of timber was a large, rough hole. A squirrel darted out from the hole and chattered noisily. On the nearby trees, birds called and sang noisily, too.

(11) "They're waiting for us to leave so they can eat," smiled Mr. Gonzalez. "Those ants and slugs may not seem tasty to us, but they are a gourmet treat for the birds."

(12) "Let's go," said Miguel. "They look hungry, and I hate making them wait for lunch."

(13) After a few minutes, Miguel turned suddenly and started walking quickly in the opposite direction, back toward the log.

(14) "Hey, what are you doing? What's up?" called Miguel's father.

(15) Miguel stopped and turned around. "We left the log uncovered. If we don't put the leaves and bark back where we found them, the ants won't have anywhere to hide."

(16) Miguel's father laughed and started to jog toward his son. "A little while ago you hated that log. Now you want to protect it."

(17) "You always told me to treat others as you want to be treated," said Miguel with a smile. "I'm just following your advice!"

Block City

by Robert Louis Stevenson

What are you able to build with your blocks?
Castles and palaces, temples and docks.
Rain may keep raining, and others go roam,
But I can be happy and building at home.

Let the sofa be mountains, the carpet the sea,
There I'll establish a city for me:
A kirk and a mill and a palace beside,
And a harbor as well where my vessels may ride.

Great is the palace with pillar and wall,
A sort of a tower on the top of it all.
And steps coming down in an orderly way
To where my toy vessels lie safe in the hay.

This one is sailing and that one is moored:
Hark to the song of the sailors on board!
And see on the steps of the palace, the kings
Coming and going with presents and things!

Now I have done with it, down let it go!
All in a moment the town is laid low.
Block upon block lying scattered and free,
What is there left of my town by the sea?

Yet as I saw it, I see it again,
The kirk and the palace, the ships and the men,
And as long as I live and where 'er I may be,
I'll always remember my town by the sea.

Refer to the passage "Miguel's World" to answer questions 8-12.

8. Paragraph 1 is mostly about:

a. The woods near Miguel's house
b. Miguel's father's love for nature
c. Miguel's behavior during walks
d. How sticks can be used as weapons

9. Which meaning best fits the way the word *identify* is used in paragraph 2?

a. To become the same
b. To understand well
c. To recognize
d. To symbolize

10. Why were the birds in paragraph 10 making so much noise?

a. Miguel messed up their nest.
b. Miguel kicked the log.
c. They wanted to eat the bugs that Miguel had uncovered in the log.
d. The squirrel was making noise, and they wanted to be louder.

11. Which sentence from the story showed that Miguel changed his mind?

a. "You always told me to treat others as you want to be treated"
b. "A little while ago you hated that log. Now you want to protect it."
c. "They look hungry, and I hate making them wait for lunch."
d. "If we don't put the leaves and bark back where we found them, the ants won't have anywhere to hide."

12. What will Miguel probably do from now on if he comes across a log in the trail? Write your response on the lines below. Include evidence from the passage to support your response.

____

____

____

____

Refer to the passage "Block City" to answer questions 13-15.

13. Reread stanzas 2 and 3. What do these stanzas describe?

a. They describe what inspired the speaker to build the city.
b. They describe how the speaker feels about the city.
c. They describe what the speaker does once he has built the city.
d. They describe the city that the speaker builds with the blocks.

14. Reread the first stanza:

What are you able to build with your blocks?
Castles and palaces, temples and docks.
Rain may keep raining, and others go roam,
But I can be happy and building at home.

Which of the following is correct about the poet's word choice and voice in this stanza?

a. The words *blocks* and *rain* show that the poet is disappointed that he must play with blocks.
b. The words *what* and *can* show that the poet is confused about how to play with blocks.
c. The words *able* and *happy* show that the poet is glad he gets to play with blocks.
d. The words *keep* and *roam* show that the poet is tired of playing with blocks.

15. What is the poet's purpose for writing this poem?

a. To persuade the reader to play with blocks
b. To describe why and how the speaker enjoys playing with blocks
c. To give the reader instructions for playing with blocks
d. To explain how the speaker discovered that he likes playing with blocks

Refer to the passages "Miguel's World" and "Block City" to answer questions 16-18.

16. What is one way that the ants' log and the speaker's city are similar?

a. The log and the city both have many pieces.
b. The log and the city are both made from rotting wood.
c. The log and the city were both made by a young child.
d. The log and the city are both disrupted at some point.

17. What is one difference between the ants in the story and the speaker in the poem?

a. The ants built the log, while the speaker did not build the city.
b. The ants live in the log, while the speaker does not live in the city.
c. The ants do not share the log with other creatures, while the speaker shares the city with other children.
d. The ants can easily move the log, while the speaker cannot easily move the city.

18. Which of the following describes a difference between Miguel and the speaker in the poem?

a. Miguel goes through a change in the story. The speaker of the poem does not go through a change in the poem.
b. Miguel decides that he cares about the ants. The speaker decides that he dislikes his blocks.
c. Miguel is in the woods by himself. The speaker of the poem is with the people living in the city.
d. Miguel has a big imagination. The speaker of the poem does not have an imagination.

An Unforgettable Day at the History Museum

(1) Hakeem's third-grade class takes a field trip every spring to the county historical museum. The county historian gives the class a tour and, afterward, sets the students loose to explore the museum. Hakeem's older brother, Gerard, went two years earlier. Gerard said the museum was great, except for one room.

(2) "Watch out for the room with the old war uniforms; it's haunted," said Gerard at dinner one night.

(3) "What do you mean, haunted?" asked Hakeem.

(4) "We heard funny noises in the room," said Gerard. "We looked around to see if anyone else was there, but it was empty. Then, Sammy swore he saw the eyes of one of the costume dummies move around, as if it were watching us. We were so scared that we left before we got to the end of the exhibit."

(5) "Gerard, stop scaring your brother," said Hakeem's mother. "Hakeem, there is no such thing as ghosts. I'm sure there is a logical explanation for those noises. As for the eyes moving, that's just Sammy's imagination getting out of hand."

(6) Stories about ghosts usually do not frighten Hakeem. He laughed at all the ghost stories his counselor told at camp last summer around the campfire. He watched scary movies with his babysitter and felt fine. But something about Gerard's words made Hakeem feel uneasy. Gerard does not usually joke around. Hakeem doubted that Gerard was just trying to scare him. Instead, Gerard was probably trying to warn him.

(7) On the day of the field trip, Hakeem asked his teacher, Mr. Orwell, about Gerard's story as they rode the bus to the museum.

(8) "It's an old building," said Mr. Orwell. "The floorboards creak, and I'm sure there are other parts of the museum that make strange noises. It's not haunted, just a little creepy."

(9) "What about the eyes watching Sammy?" asked Hakeem.

(10) Mr. Orwell laughed. "Sammy's got a great imagination," he said. "I'm sure that's what made him think the statue was watching him."

(11) After the tour, Hakeem walked around the museum with his best friend, Malcolm. Malcolm wanted to see the old war uniforms, but Hakeem was nervous. Finally, he agreed to follow his friend into the room. There were just a few standing lamps and one small bulb on the ceiling to provide light. Ten life-size dummies, or mannequins, each one wearing a different war uniform, stood in the dim room. As Hakeem walked by a mannequin, the overhead light flickered. At that moment, Hakeem looked at the mannequin's face. The flickering light made the shadows over its eyes jump. Hakeem gasped.

(12) "What is it?" asked Malcolm.

(13) "Watch," said Hakeem. They stood in front of the mannequin and waited. After a minute, the light overhead flickered.

(14) "Whoa!" said Malcolm. "That looked like he was shifting his eyes!"

(15) "That explains what Sammy saw," said Hakeem. "What about the noises?"

(16) Malcolm started leaning from side to side and walked around the room like a duck. Each time he shifted his weight to one side, a floorboard creaked. As he wobbled around the room, the floorboards creaked and moaned.

(17) "This place is great!" Hakeem said. He laughed and added, "I'm so glad my brother didn't scare me away!

Refer to the passage "An Unforgettable Day at the History Museum" to answer questions 19-24.

19. This question has two parts. After you answer Part A, answer Part B:

Part A: Which statement from the passage shows that Hakeem's mother does not trust Sammy's description of the dummy?

a. "Gerard, stop scaring your brother."
b. "Hakeem, there is no such thing as ghosts"
c. "I'm sure there is a logical explanation for those noises."
d. "That's just Sammy's imagination getting out of hand."

Part B: Who else in the story says the same thing as Hakeem's mother regarding Sammy's description?

a. Gerard
b. Mr. Orwell
c. Malcolm
d. Hakeem

20. Why did Hakeem laugh in paragraph 17?

a. Because Malcolm walked like a duck in the old uniform room
b. Because the old uniform room was haunted
c. Because his brother, Gerard, lied to him about the old uniform room
d. Because he found out the old uniform room was not haunted

21. Which of the following statements describes a theme of this story?

a. Imagination is dangerous
b. Appearances can be deceiving
c. Trust people older than you
d. Historical museums are haunted

22. How is the story's plot impacted by the setting of the old museum?

a. The museum exhibits inspire Hakeem to open his own museum one day.
b. The quiet and dim museum led Hakeem to become bored and uncomfortable.
c. There are illusions and sounds in the museum that make Hakeem nervous.
d. The displays in the museum tempt Hakeem to steal pieces from the exhibits.

23. Which of the following describes Malcolm's attitude toward Hakeem?

a. Malcolm does not care that Hakeem is scared.
b. Malcolm is afraid that Hakeem will laugh at him for enjoying the museum.
c. Malcolm is upset at Hakeem being scared and thinks he is silly.
d. Malcolm is patient with Hakeem as Hakeem faces his fear.

24. Which of the following describes the main conflict of the story?

a. Hakeem is afraid to go into the room in the museum that may be haunted.
b. Hakeem wants to prove his brother wrong about the room he said was haunted.
c. Hakeem is afraid that Malcolm will want to go in the haunted room in the museum.
d. Hakeem wants to get back at his brother for scaring him about the room at the museum.

Extended Response

Your STAAR test will include the following instructions for your extended response question. The response prompts used here are similar to the prompts you will see on the STAAR test.

25. Read the selection "An Unforgettable Day at the History Museum." Based on the information in the selection, write a response to the following:

Explain how Hakeem acts with bravery in the story.

Write a well-organized informational essay that uses specific evidence from the selection to support your answer.

Remember to —

- clearly state your central idea
- organize your writing
- develop your ideas in detail
- use evidence from the selection in your response
- use correct spelling, capitalization, punctuation, and grammar

Manage your time carefully so that you can —

- review the selection
- plan your response
- write your response
- revise and edit your response

Revising

Chandler wrote the following paper about volcanoes. Read the following paper and note the revisions that Chandler should make. Once you have read his paper, answer the questions that follow it.

The Power of Volcanoes

(1) The word *volcano* comes from *Vulcan*, the name of the ancient Roman god of fire. (2) A volcano occurs when hot, melted rock, called magma, breaks through the earth's crust. (3) I once saw a volcano erupt when I was on vacation in Hawaii. (4) When magma comes out on the surface of the earth, it is called lava. (5) Hot lava and ash often explode out of volcanoes, sometimes causing a lot of destruction.

(6) There are four basic types of volcanoes. (7) Shield volcanoes have broad slopes. (8) Shield volcanoes also have gentle slopes. (8) Cinder cone volcanoes are pointed, kind of like pyramids. (9) Strato-volcanoes have many layers of rock formed by hardened lava and ash from previous eruptions. (10) Dome volcanoes are shaped like steep mounds and are the result of slow-flowing lava.

(11) Whatever the type, volcanoes happen in places where one of the plates of the earth's crust touches another. (12) There are many active volcanoes all over the place. (13) Some are in the United States, in places like Washington, Colorado, and Hawaii. (14) Some volcanoes are even under water, far below the surface of the ocean.

(15) When volcanoes erupt, they can change many things. (16) They can add height to mountains and even form new islands. (17) In Iceland, the island of Surtsey was formed by an erupting volcano in 1963. (18) Volcanoes can also cause mountains to collapse. (19) At Crater Lake in Oregon, a volcano collapsed a mountain, forming the deepest lake in the United States. (20) No matter their effects, volcanic eruptions can be very powerful.

26. Which sentence does not belong in paragraph 1?

a. Sentence 1
b. Sentence 3
c. Sentence 4
d. Sentence 5

27. Sentences 7 and 8 can be combined. Please write one sentence that states the information given in sentences 7 and 8. Write the new sentence on the lines below.

____

____

____

28. Another sentence can be added at the end of paragraph 3. Which of the following sentences would be the best sentence to add there?

a. Though there are some mountains in North Dakota, no one has ever found a volcano there.
b. When underwater volcanoes erupt, islands may form from the lava that cools at the water's surface.
c. If there is a volcano in your state, you should know what to do in case it erupts.
d. No matter where a volcano is located, it can still erupt and have a long-lasting impact on the area.

29. The phrase "all over the place" in sentence 12 is not very clear. Which of the following phrases should replace this phrase?

a. All around
b. All over the world
c. In different places
d. In the oceans

David wrote the following paper about his favorite author. Read the following paper and note the revisions that David should make. Once you have read his paper, answer the questions that follow it.

C.S. Lewis

(1) Clive Staples Lewis is known as C.S. Lewis. (2) He is famous for writing a book series called *The Chronicles of Narnia*. (3) C.S. Lewis was born in Northern Ireland and lived there for part of his childhood. (4) When he was older, he was sent to school in England. (5) At first, C.S. Lewis did not want to live in England. (6) However, he stayed there for most of his life.

(7) C.S. Lewis learned from tutors and attended multiple schools. (8) As he studied and grew up, he read many books, stories, myths, and poems. (9) He was very interested in some of the stories he read. (10) These stories inspired him, and he started making up things. (11) He continued coming up with stories as an adult and had them published as books for others to read. (12) Many people liked his books, and he became a popular writer.

(13) He also became well known for writing nonfiction books. (14) People enjoyed these books so much that C.S. Lewis was invited to share more of his thoughts on the radio for a while during the 1940s. (15) C.S. Lewis was also a teacher at one of the schools he had attended as a student. (16) He performed well as a student, and he continued to do well as a teacher.

(17) C.S. Lewis was also inspired during his early career as an author and a teacher. (18) Later in the 1940s, C.S. Lewis began writing *The Lion, the Witch, and the Wardrobe*. (19) This was his first book for children. (20) Many of the main characters in the story were inspired by people he had met, but some were inspired by things he saw every day at the school he worked at! (21) *The Lion, the Witch, and the Wardrobe* was the first book in the series called *The Chronicles of Narnia*. (22) This series became C.S. Lewis's most famous work, and it would not have been the same without the things that inspired him to write it.

(23) C.S. Lewis continued teaching and writing for a long time. (24) He wrote another fiction book for adults after he finished writing *The Chronicles of Narnia*. (25) Even though it was not as well-known as his other books, that book was one of his favorite books he had written. (26) Much later, *The Chronicles of Narnia* were made into movies. (27) These movies helped readers enjoy the story in a new way.

(28) C.S. Lewis's books, especially *The Chronicles of Narnia*, are still popular today among both children and adults. (29) His work has inspired countless other writers to write their own stories. (30) His stories will continue to entertain and inspire readers for years to come.

30. Which sentence could be added to the end of paragraph 1 to show the central idea of the passage?

a. Throughout the rest of his life, C.S. Lewis tried to find a way to move back to Northern Ireland.
b. C.S. Lewis's life in England led him to have a successful career as a teacher and an author.
c. England is near Northern Ireland, and both countries are part of the United Kingdom.
d. C.S. Lewis spent his adult life in England, even though he was not excited to live there.

31. The word *things* in sentence 10 is not very clear. Which of the following sentences is the best revision of sentence 10?

a. These stories inspired him, and he started making up new languages.
b. These stories inspired him, and he started making up imaginary friends.
c. These stories inspired him, and he started making up his own stories.
d. These stories inspired him, and he started making up new authors.

32. Which of the following sentences could be added before sentence 13 as an introductory sentence to paragraph 3?

a. C.S. Lewis quit writing fiction books and decided to only write nonfiction books.
b. His most successful books were in a series of children's books.
c. C.S. Lewis read many nonfiction books during his life.
d. Writing fiction books is not the only thing C.S. Lewis is known for.

33. Which of the following would be best to add after sentence 13?

a. These books were not as exciting as his fiction books because they did not include imaginary characters.
b. Even though these books are nonfiction, they are written in a way that can still be fun to read.
c. In some of his nonfiction books, he mentioned other authors' books that he liked.
d. One of his closest friends was also very well known for writing fiction books.

Editing

Cassie is writing an essay about bees. Read the first two paragraphs of Cassie's essay and look for errors that she needs to correct. Once you have read the paragraphs, answer the questions that follow them.

Beautiful Bees

(1) Do you think bees are scary? (2) Next time you see one, do not fear! (3) Not all bees had stingers, and bees that do will probably not sting you. (4) Bees are very important. (5) Without bees, we would not have honey or see many flowers outside. (6) Each kind of bee has a different job to do. (7) Bees are called many different name, but the type of bee you probably see the most is a honeybee.

(8) Honeybees help new flowers grow. (9) Honeybees are attracted to the bright colors on flower petals. (10) They also get their food from flowers. (11) When a honeybee lands on a flower, pollen from the flower sticks to the bee. (12) Pollen is a yellow powder that are needed for new flowers to be made. (13) However, some flowers cannot use their own pollen to make new flowers. (14) After a bee lands on a flower and picks up pollen, it can fly to another flower and drop the pollen their. (15) By doing this, bees help new flowers grow all around us.

34. Choose the word that should replace *had* in sentence 3.

Not all bees ___________ stingers, and bees that do will probably not sting you.

have
has
were having
did have

35. Which change would correct the mistake in sentence 7?

a. Change *are* to *were.*
b. Change *name* to *names.*
c. Change *see* to *seen.*
d. Change *honeybee* to *Honeybee.*

36. Which change needs to be made to sentence 12?

a. Change *powder* to *pouder.*
b. Change *are* to *is.*
c. Add a comma after *powder.*
d. No change is needed.

37. Which change would correct the mistake in sentence 14?

a. Change *picks* to *pick.*
b. Change *to* to *from.*
c. Change *drop* to *dropped.*
d. Change *their* to *there.*

Logan is writing an essay about preparing for a hurricane. Read the first paragraph of Logan's essay and look for errors that he needs to correct. Once you have read the paragraph, answer the questions that follow them.

Preparing for Hurricanes

(1) People who live near the ocean may experience storms called hurricanes. (2) Hurricanes can cause lots of strong winds and heavy rain. (3) They usually form above the ocean during the summer. (4) This is because the air right above the ocean is warm, for the air higher in the sky is cold. (5) Hot air rises, so the air near the ocean rises. (6) Then, nearby air replaces the warm air near the ocean. (7) That air heats up and rises, and the process continuse. (8) This also causes large clouds to form, and, over time, a hurricane is created. (9) The hurricane may move through the ocean and usually shrink and fade away, but it may grow bigger and move toward land. (10) Hurricanes can cause a lot of damage to the buildings in an area. (11) If a hurricane is traveling forward your hometown, it is important to be prepared and know what to do.

38. Which change would correct the mistake in sentence 4?

a. Change *is* to *was.*
b. Change *for* to *but.*
c. Change *sky* to *Sky.*
d. Change *higher* to *highest.*

39. Which change needs to be made to sentence 7?

a. Change *heats* to *heat.*
b. Remove the comma after *rises.*
c. Change *continuse* to *continues.*
d. No change is needed.

40. Which change would correct the mistake in sentence 9?

a. Change *through* to *by.*
b. Change *usually* to *eventually.*
c. Change *grow* to *grew.*
d. Change *move* to *moved.*

41. Which change would correct the mistake in sentence 11?

a. Change *forward* to *toward.*
b. Change *your* to *you.*
c. Add a comma after *prepared.*
d. Change *know* to *knew.*

Answer Key and Explanations for Test #1

Reading

1. C: TEKS Standard (3.3)(D)

Paragraph 2 says that, when Neil Armstrong was 14, his family moved back to Wapakoneta permanently. In the sentence before that, it says that the family moved 20 times. The word *permanently* shows that something changed about how often the family moved. The passage also does not say that the family moved again. This shows that *permanent* must mean "for good," since the Armstrong family stayed in Wapakoneta for good. The passage does not show that the Armstrong family needed to be in Wapakoneta by a certain day, so choice A is incorrect. The passage also does not say what time of day they moved, so choice B is incorrect. The passage does not mention other events that happened when the Armstrong family moved, so choice D is incorrect.

2. C: TEKS Standard (3.10)(C)

The section title "First Man on the Moon" shows that the section under that title is about Neil Armstrong being in the group of astronauts that walked on the moon. The year that Neil Armstrong walked on the moon is the most likely detail to be included in this section. The high school Neil Armstrong went to and the number of siblings he had would most likely be mentioned in the section titled "Armstrong's Childhood." This means choices A and D are incorrect. Choice B is not related to Neil Armstrong walking on the moon, so choice B is also incorrect.

3. D: TEKS Standard (3.9)(Diii)

This passage tells events in chronological order. It describes how Neil's childhood and early career led him to work for NASA and go to the moon. This means choice D is correct. The passage does not describe the history of NASA. It only mentions the year that NASA was created, so choice A is incorrect. The passage does not talk about Neil Armstrong's teachers or how he learned to fly a spaceship. Choices B and C are incorrect.

4. B: TEKS Standard (3.9)(Dii)

These titles use words and phrases like *childhood*, *career*, and *later life*. These words and phrases are related to parts of Neil Armstrong's life. The text under each section title describes the events that took place during a certain part of his life. Choice B is correct. Choice A is incorrect because only the section "Armstrong's Childhood" tells where he lived. Choice C is incorrect because the section "Armstrong's Childhood" does not talk about Neil Armstrong having a job. Choice D is incorrect because the passage only talks about one of Neil Armstrong's missions.

5. C: TEKS Standard (3.3)(A)

Paragraph 3 says that Neil Armstrong started college at Purdue University but stopped to join the military. It says that, later, he "came back to finish his college degree." This means that he finished his classes at college and was able to graduate from Purdue. In this sentence, *degree* is used to show that he finished college. This paragraph does not talk about heat or angles, so choices A and D are incorrect. Choice C is incorrect because *degree* is not being used to describe something in this sentence.

6. A: TEKS Standard (3.6)(G)

Paragraph 5 describes what Neil Armstrong did after he worked for NASA as an astronaut. It says he chose to become a professor instead of enjoying his fame. Choice A is correct, since this paragraph describes Neil Armstrong choosing a humble life. The paragraph does not say that Neil Armstrong was shy or that he did not know about politics, so choices B and C are incorrect. Choice D is incorrect because Neil Armstrong was a successful astronaut and is still remembered today.

7. B: TEKS Standard (3.6)(H)

The passage talks about Neil Armstrong's accomplishments and says that his life was "out of this world." This supports the conclusion that he will be remembered as a historical figure, so choice B is correct. The passage does not say that other astronauts must have a degree or pilot's license, so choice A is incorrect. It also does not mention any astronauts walking on the moon since Neil Armstrong and his team, so choice C is incorrect. The passage does not talk about Neil Armstrong and President Kennedy meeting or becoming friends, so choice D is incorrect.

8. C: TEKS Standard (3.6)(G)

Paragraph 1 describes how Miguel acted during walks when he was younger. The paragraph mentions that Miguel and his father walked in the woods near their house. However, the paragraph does not describe the woods, so choice A is incorrect. The paragraph also does not describe how Miguel's father feels about nature, so choice B is incorrect. While the paragraph says that Miguel pretended the sticks were weapons, this is just a detail in the paragraph. This means choice D is incorrect.

9. C: TEKS Standard (3.3)(B)

In paragraph 2, the passage says that Miguel's father told Miguel how to identify trees. He explained that looking at the trees' leaves and bark would help him do this. In this sentence, *identify* means to recognize. Miguel's father is teaching Miguel how to look at a tree and recognize what kind of tree it is, so choice C is correct. It would not make sense for Miguel to become the same as the trees, so choice A is incorrect. By looking at the bark and leaves on a tree, Miguel can know what kind of tree it is, and he might be able to make some inferences about the tree. However, these things do not help Miguel understand the tree well, so choice B is incorrect. Miguel's father does not teach Miguel how to create a symbol for the tree, so choice D is incorrect.

10. C: TEKS Standard (3.6)(F)

After the birds began making noise, Miguel's father says that they are waiting until they can eat. He then says that the ants would be tasty to the birds. These comments show that the birds want to eat the bugs on the log, so choice C is correct. Miguel did not mess up the birds' nest, so choice A is incorrect. The birds did not begin making noise when Miguel kicked the log, so choice B is incorrect. There is nothing in the passage that shows the birds wanting to make more noise than the squirrel. This means choice D is incorrect.

11. B: TEKS Standard (3.7)(C)

Choice B is from Miguel's father's dialogue in paragraph 16. In this statement, Miguel's father is observing that Miguel's behavior has changed. He says that Miguel hated the log before, but that he has changed and now thinks it should be protected. The statement in choice A shows why Miguel wants to protect the log. However, it does not show that he has changed his mind. The statement in choice C shows that Miguel does not want to get in the way of the birds finding food. Choice D shows that he then wants to give the ants a chance to hide from the birds. Neither of these statements, by themselves, show that Miguel changed his mind. They simply explain the reason for his actions.

12. TEKS Standard (3.6)(C)

Miguel will most likely leave the log alone, or he will look for bugs or other animals in the log. At the end of the story, Miguel says that he wants to follow his father's advice to treat others as he would want to be treated. He also shows that he cares about the ants when he goes back to help them hide from the bird that will eat them. These events from the story show that Miguel has respect for the creatures that live in the woods. He does not want to hurt them or disturb them like he did early in the passage.

13. D: TEKS Standard (3.9)(B)

These stanzas show that the city the speaker built had a mill, a harbor, ships, and a palace with a pillar, wall, tower, and steps. This is a description of the city, so choice D is correct. The speaker does not describe his feelings about the city. The speaker also does not say what inspired him to build it. This means that choices A and B are incorrect. The poem says that the speaker later knocked down the city, but this is described in stanza 5. This means choice C is incorrect.

14. C: TEKS Standard (3.10)(F)

Throughout the poem, the speaker mentions that he enjoys building with blocks. In the first stanza, he says he is happy when he is building things with blocks. He also asks the readers what they are able to build. This shows that the speaker thinks building with blocks is something he has the privilege to do. This means choice C is correct. The speaker does not use words in the poem to show that he is bored, confused, or tired. He only describes building with blocks as a fun activity, so choices A, B, and D are incorrect.

15. B: TEKS Standard (3.10)(A)

The poet uses a young speaker in this poem. The speaker describes a city made of blocks. The speaker also says that building with blocks is a fun activity that he is happy to do. This fits the purpose described in choice B, so it is the correct choice. While the speaker describes playing with blocks as a fun activity, the speaker does not tell the audience to play with blocks. This makes choice A incorrect. The speaker does not explain the steps for building a block city, so choice C is incorrect. The speaker of the poem has played with blocks before, so choice D is incorrect.

16. D: TEKS Standard (3.6)(E)

In "Miguel's World," Miguel kicks the log, which disrupts the log and the animals inside. In "Block City," the speaker disrupts the city by knocking it down. Choice D is correct. In "Miguel's World," the log only has a few pieces: bark, leaves, and wood. The log is not made of many pieces, so choice A is incorrect. The blocks in “Block City” are probably made of wood, but the poem does not say or show that they are rotten. This means choice B is incorrect. The log in "Miguel's World" was not made by a child. It was made naturally, so choice D is also incorrect.

17. B:TEKS Standard (3.6)(E)

In "Miguel's World," Miguel's father explains that the ants live in the log. However, the speaker in "Block City" only built the city made of blocks. The speaker does not live in the city. The ants in "Miguel's World" did not build the log, so choice A is incorrect. The ants share the log with other creatures. The speaker in "Block City" does not mention sharing the city with others. Choice C is incorrect. The ants in "Miguel's World" could not move the log without help. The speaker in "Block City" built the city without help. Choice D is also incorrect.

18. A: TEKS Standard (3.6)(E)

In "Miguel's World," Miguel changes his mind about how he will treat the things and creatures in the forest. In "Block City," the speaker does not change how he feels about playing with blocks. This means choice A is correct. Since the speaker never shows that he dislikes blocks, choice B is also incorrect. In "Miguel's World," Miguel is walking in the woods with his father, so choice C is incorrect. "Miguel's World" does not show Miguel using his imagination. In "Block City," the speaker uses his imagination to build a city and think about what people would do in the city. This means choice D is incorrect.

19. TEKS Standard (3.7)(C)

Part A: D: Choice D is a statement Hakeem's mother's makes in paragraph 5. In this statement, Hakeem's mother says that Sammy imagined that the statue's eyes were moving. She is saying that his description is incorrect. The statements in choices A, B, and C do not show what Hakeem's mother thinks of Sammy's description of the dummy. Choice A shows that she wants Gerard to stop telling Hakeem things that will scare him. Choice B shows that she does not believe in ghosts. Choice C shows that she thinks the noises were caused by something other than a ghost.

Part B: B: In paragraph 10, Mr. Orwell says, "Sammy's got a great imagination," and, "I'm sure that's what made him think the statue was watching him." This statement shows that Mr. Orwell and Hakeem's mother have the same opinion about Sammy's description. Choice A is incorrect because Gerard believes Sammy's description. Choice C is incorrect because Malcolm does not say anything about whether or not he believes Sammy's description. Choice D is incorrect because Hakeem believes Sammy's description. At the end, Hakeem realizes that Sammy did not understand what he had seen. Hakeem did not say that Sammy had imagined that the statue's eyes were moving.

20. D: TEKS Standard (3.6)(F)

Hakeem laughed because he found out that what his brother thought were ghosts were actually just creaking floorboards and a flickering bulb. He laughed because there was a logical explanation for the scary parts of the room. Choice A is incorrect because Hakeem does not laugh as Malcolm walks around like a duck. Choice B is incorrect because the room was not haunted. Choice C is incorrect because Gerard did not lie to Hakeem. Gerard did think that the room was haunted, but he was wrong.

21. B: TEKS Standard (3.8)(A)

This story shows that appearances can be deceiving. The creaking floorboards and jumping shadows misled Gerard into thinking a ghost was in the room. What Gerard thought he saw turned out to be something completely different and safe. Choice A is incorrect because the story does not show that imagination is dangerous. Choice C is incorrect because Gerard and Sammy are older than Hakeem, but they were not trustworthy. Choice D is incorrect because the museum in this story was not actually haunted.

22. C: TEKS Standard (3.8)(D)

The problem Hakeem experiences in this story is that he is afraid to go into the war uniforms room of a museum. His brother tells him that strange things happened in that room, so Hakeem wants to avoid it during his field trip. If this story had a different setting, then the events and Hakeem's problem would be different. Choice A is incorrect because Hakeem does not show interest in opening a museum. Choices B and D are incorrect because the passage does not say or show that Hakeem is bored or tempted to steal.

23. D: TEKS Standard (3.8)(B)

Malcolm wants to go into the old war uniform room, but Hakeem is hesitant. The passage does not say that Malcolm pressured or made fun of Hakeem for being scared. Malcolm also listens to Hakeem and waits with him to see the light flicker on the statue. He also helps Hakeem find out where the noises are coming from. This shows that he is patient with Hakeem. Choices A and C are incorrect because Malcolm does not react to Hakeem being scared. Instead, he actually helps him understand why he should not be scared. Choice B is incorrect because Malcolm never mentions being nervous that Hakeem will mock him.

24. A: TEKS Standard (3.8)(C)

The main problem in this story is that Hakeem becomes scared of a room in the museum he is visiting on a field trip. Choice B is incorrect because Hakeem believes that his brother is right about the room. Choice C is incorrect because Hakeem does not think about Malcolm wanting to visit the room until Malcolm says he wants to visit it. Choice D is incorrect because Hakeem never mentions wanting to get revenge on his brother.

Extended Response

25. TEKS Standard (3.7)(B)

Please use the rubric below to make sure your response meets these common criteria. Try to have a friend or family member grade your response for you or take a break after writing your response and return to grade it yourself with fresh eyes.

Below is an excerpt of the STAAR Grades 3-5 Informational Writing Rubric.

<table>
<tr><th>Score Point</th><th>Organization and Development of Ideas</th></tr>
<tr><td>3</td><td>
<ul>
<li>Central idea is clear and fully developed
The central idea is clearly identifiable. The focus is consistent throughout, creating a response that is unified and easy to follow.</li>
<li>Organization is effective
A purposeful structure that includes an effective introduction and conclusion is evident. The organizational structure is appropriate and effectively supports the development of the central idea. The sentences, paragraphs, or ideas are logically connected in purposeful and highly effective ways.</li>
<li>Evidence is specific, well chosen, and relevant
The response includes relevant text-based evidence that is clearly explained and consistently supports and develops the central idea. For pairs in grades 3-5, evidence is drawn from at least one text. The response reflects a thorough understanding of the writing purpose.</li>
<li>Expression of ideas is clear and effective
The writer's word choice is specific, purposeful, and enhances the response. Almost all sentences and phrases are effectively crafted to convey the writer's ideas and contribute to the overall quality of the response and the clarity of the message.</li>
</ul>
</td></tr>
<tr><th>Score Point</th><th>Conventions</th></tr>
<tr><td>2</td><td>Student writing demonstrates consistent command of grade-level-appropriate conventions, including correct:
<ul>
<li>sentence construction</li>
<li>punctuation</li>
<li>capitalization</li>
<li>grammar</li>
<li>spelling</li>
</ul>
The response has few errors, but those errors do not impact the clarity of the writing.</td></tr>
</table>

Revising

26. B: TEKS Standard (3.11)(Bii)

This paragraph is an introduction to a report about volcanoes. The paragraph should only include information about volcanoes and how they work. Sentence 3 is off topic because it is about the author seeing a volcano. This sentence should not be used in this passage, so choice B is correct. Sentence 1 is about where the word *volcano* came from. Sentence 4 explains what lava is. Sentence 5 describes the common effects of volcanic eruptions. These are all details about volcanoes, so choices A, C, and D are incorrect.

27. TEKS Standard (3.11)(C)

The new sentence should be similar to the following sentence: Shield volcanoes have broad and gentle slopes. The sentence should mention shield volcanoes and include the details that their slopes are both broad and gentle. The sentence should also be a complete sentence and use proper grammar and spelling.

28. D: TEKS Standard (3.11)(Bi)

The purpose of a concluding sentence is to wrap up the paragraph. Sometimes, a concluding sentence will include a new detail that prepares the reader for the next paragraph. Choice D is related to the main idea of the paragraph, since it mentions the locations of volcanoes. It also mentions that many things change when volcanoes erupt. This is the main idea of the next paragraph. Choice D both concludes paragraph 3 and prepares the reader for paragraph 4. Choice A is incorrect because it only introduces a new idea. It does not cover the main idea of the paragraph. Choice B is incorrect because it only contains a new supporting detail. This supporting detail should go in paragraph 4, not paragraph 3. Choice C is incorrect because it introduces a new idea, but the new idea does not prepare the reader for the next paragraph.

29. B: TEKS Standard (3.11)(C)

The phrase "all over the place" is unclear. It does not help the reader understand that there are volcanoes around the world. Sentence 12 should say, "There are many active volcanoes all over the world." Choice B is correct because it replaces the unclear phrase with a phrase that is more specific. Choices A and C do not give the reader enough information. They are also unclear and do not show the reader that active volcanoes exist all over the world. Choice D is not the right choice because it does not give the reader the correct information. The next sentence, sentence 13, states that there are active volcanoes in Washington and Colorado. These states are not in the ocean. This detail shows that sentence 12 should not be talking about active volcanoes in the oceans, specifically.

30. B: TEKS Standard (3.11)(Bi)

Choice B shows a sentence that is related to the topic of paragraph 1. It is also related to the central idea of the passage, which is C.S. Lewis's life as an author. This makes choice B the correct choice. Choices A and D are not related to the central idea of the passage. They focus on where C.S. Lewis wanted to live, not his life as a writer. Choices A and D are incorrect. Choice C states a fact about Northern Ireland. This fact is not closely related to the central idea of the passage, so choice C is incorrect.

31. C: TEKS Standard (3.11)(C)

Sentence 10 is unclear because it says that C.S. Lewis made up things. The sentence does not help the reader understand what C.S. Lewis made up. The next sentence says that he "continued coming up with stories." This shows that C.S. Lewis had begun making up his own stories, so choice C is correct. The passage does not mention that C.S. Lewis made up new languages, imaginary friends, or new authors. Since these revisions are not supported by the passage, choices A, B, and D are incorrect.

32. D: TEKS Standard (3.11)(Bi)

An introductory sentence of a paragraph should let the reader know what the paragraph is about. The question is asking which sentence would be the best introductory sentence for the third paragraph in the passage. The paragraph is about the fact that C.S. Lewis did well as a nonfiction author, a speaker, and a teacher. Choice D is the best choice. This sentence would let the reader know that the paragraph is about the other things C.S. Lewis is known for. The passage shows that choice A is not true, so it is incorrect. Choices B and C are not related to the topic of the paragraph, so they are also incorrect.

33. B: TEKS Standard (3.11)(Bii)

Sentence 13 and sentence 14 are about how C.S. Lewis was also successful as a nonfiction writer. A sentence added after sentence 13 should be related to this topic. Choice B is the best answer because it shows why C.S. Lewis's nonfiction books were popular. Choice A is incorrect because it is a negative statement about Lewis's nonfiction. It would not fit well after sentence 13. Choice C is related to the topic of sentence 13, but it does not tell the reader information that is related to C.S. Lewis's nonfiction writing. Choice C is incorrect. Choice D is incorrect because it is off topic.

Editing

34. have: TEKS Standard (3.11)(Dii)

The question is asking which verb should be used in this sentence. The word *do* shows that this sentence is in the present tense. The word *bees* also shows that the correct verb will go with a plural noun. *Have* is a present tense verb that is used with plural nouns, so it is the correct choice. *Has* is used with singular nouns, so it is incorrect. *Were having* and *did have* would not be used in present tense. These choices are also incorrect.

35. B: TEKS Standard (3.11)(Diii)

The sentence says that "bees are called many different name." The word *many* shows that the sentence is talking about more than one name. The plural noun, *names*, should be used in this sentence, so choice B is correct. The verbs *were* and *seen* are past tense verbs, but this sentence is in present tense. Choices A and C are incorrect. In this sentence, the *honeybee* is used to name a type of bee. Names of types of animals are not proper nouns, so choice D is incorrect.

36. B: TEKS Standard (3.11)(Di)

The sentence says that "pollen is a yellow powder." Powder is a singular noun, so it should be used with singular verbs. The verb *are* is a plural verb. The verb *is* is singular and should be used instead, so choice B is correct. The word *powder* is spelled correctly, so choice A is incorrect. A comma is not needed after the word *powder* in this sentence, so choice C is incorrect. Since *are* is used incorrectly and should be changed to *is*, choice D is incorrect.

37. D: TEKS Standard (3.2)(Bii)

The words *their* and *there* are homophones. *Their is* a possessive pronoun that is used to show ownership. *There* is a pronoun that is used to replace the name of a specific place or location. This sentence talks about the places that bees drop pollen, so *there* is the correct word to use. Choice D is correct. The word *bee* is singular, so it should be used with a singular noun. *Picks* is a singular verb, so choice A is incorrect. The sentence says that a bee can fly from one flower and then fly toward another flower. *To* is used to show that something is going toward something else, but *from* is used to show that it is going away. This means the bee flies to another flower, so choice B is incorrect. The verb *dropped* is a past tense verb. This sentence is not in the past tense, so choice C is incorrect.

38. B: TEKS Standard (3.11)(Dviii)

This sentence uses the wrong coordinating conjunction. The first part of the sentence says the air above the ocean is warm. The second part of the sentence says the air that is higher than that is cold. The two types of air are not alike, so the sentence should show that they are different. The word *for* should be changed to *but. For* shows that one thing is the reason for another. *But* shows that two ideas are different, so it is the correct choice. Choice A is incorrect because changing *is* to *was* would add a past tense verb where a present tense verb is needed. Choice C is incorrect because *sky* is not a proper noun. It does not need to be capitalized. Choice D is incorrect because *higher* is used to compare two things, but *highest* is used to compare more than two things. Only two types of air are being compared, so *higher* is the correct word to use.

39. C: TEKS Standard (3.2)(Biv)

The word *continues* is misspelled in sentence 7, so choice C is correct. This word is spelled using a vowel team instead of a silent *e. Heats* is a verb that goes with a singular noun used in present tense. The sentence correctly uses the word *heats*, so choice A is incorrect. This sentence is a compound sentence, so it should include a comma and a coordinating conjunction. The comma after *rises* should not be removed, so choice B is incorrect. There is a spelling mistake in this sentence, so choice D is incorrect.

40. B: TEKS Standard (3.11)(Dv)

Usually means that something happens often. The sentence says that a hurricane may move through the ocean, but it does not say this happens often. The word *usually* does not make sense in this sentence. The word *eventually* would make sense. This word would show that after a hurricane moves through the ocean, it will shrink over time. Choice B is correct. The hurricane moves across the water, not next to it, so choice A is incorrect. The sentence is not in past tense, and the words *grew* and *moved* are used in past tense. Choices C and D are incorrect.

41. A: TEKS Standard (3.2)(Bvi)

The word *forward* is used to show that something moves to the area in front of it. The word *toward* is used to show that something moves to be in the same area as something else. The word *toward* should be used to replace the word *forward* in sentence 11, so choice A is correct. The sentence uses a possessive pronoun, *your*, before the word *hometown*. Since this is talking about the reader's hometown, a possessive pronoun is correct. Choice B is incorrect. There is no need for a comma after the word *prepared* in this sentence, so choice C is incorrect. The word *knew* is a past tense verb. This sentence is not in the past tense, so choice D is wrong.

Practice Test #2

Reading

Our Neighbor Mercury

(1) Earth is a planet with many neighbors. Besides Earth, there are seven other full-sized planets in the solar system, and the one that is the closest to the Sun is named Mercury. Earth is about two and a half times the size of Mercury. The surface of Mercury is very rough, like our moon. There are lots of craters, and it is completely barren, with nothing but soil as far as the eye can see. Do you know how Mercury got its name? The name comes from Ancient Rome, some 24 centuries ago. The Romans believed in many different gods, and the messenger of the gods was called Mercury. He was able to move extremely fast. Because this planet moves around the Sun faster than the other planets, it was given the name Mercury.

(2) Sometimes, Mercury is closer to our planet than at other times, but it is always a long way away. The closest it ever gets to us is about 40 million miles. It is much closer to the Sun than Earth is, so it doesn't take nearly as long to revolve around the Sun. In fact, it only takes 88 days for Mercury to orbit the Sun. Here on Earth, a year is 365 days long, but, on Mercury, a year is only 88 days long. This means that if you're 10 years old on Earth, you would be almost 42 years old if you lived on Mercury!

(3) If that's not strange enough, consider this: Earth orbits around the Sun, and it also rotates, like a spinning top. One full rotation is 24 hours, or one day. Mercury also rotates, but much more slowly. A day on Mercury is 58 Earth days. Since a year on Mercury is only 88 Earth days, that means there are only one and a half "days" in a Mercury year. That would be like the Sun coming up on Earth and then it being sunny 24 hours a day for four months, and then dark for four months straight, and then sunny again for four months. That would be very hard to get used to. Living on Mercury, where a day is 58 Earth days long, would be quite a change.

(4) Of course, there's no chance that anyone will ever actually live on Mercury. It's impossible due to the temperatures on the planet. Temperatures can range from 300 degrees below zero to around 800 degrees. 800 degrees is hot enough to melt some metals. We would broil to death almost instantly on Mercury. When it got

dark, we would freeze to death. Some people believe that, one of these days, an astronaut will walk on Mars, but that will never happen on Mercury!

Refer to the passage "Our Neighbor Mercury" to answer questions 1-6.

1. What is the main purpose of this passage?

a. To explain how long a year is
b. To discuss the entire solar system
c. To give facts about the Sun
d. To give facts about the planet Mercury

2. What word below means the same thing as barren **in paragraph 1?**

a. Blue
b. Round
c. Lifeless
d. Gigantic

3. In paragraph 1, what does *Ancient* mean?

a. Far away
b. Very old
c. Recent
d. Fictional

4. Why do you think it gets so much hotter on Mercury than on Earth? Write your answer on the lines below. Include evidence from the passage to support your response.

____

____

____

____

5. Which of the following statements describes the main idea of paragraph 4?

a. One day on Mercury is almost as long as one day on Earth.
b. Humans cannot survive on Mercury due to the temperatures.
c. Mercury is extremely hot because it is so close to the Sun.
d. Mercury only has two seasons: summer and winter.

6. Which of the following is true about the diagram of the solar system?

a. The author included the diagram to show how Mercury was discovered.
b. The author included the diagram to show why Mercury is named *Mercury*.
c. The author included the diagram to show how close Mercury is to the Sun.
d. The author included the diagram to show what life would be like on Mercury.

Fire Needs Fuel and More to Burn

(1) On the ground lay a dead tree, its branches sticking out like a porcupine's quills. Jake started breaking off the branches and putting them in a pile. His father had sent him to find kindling wood for their fire.

(2) "What's kindling wood?" Jake had asked.

(3) "Boy! You've been living in the city too long, Jake!" answered Jake's father. "Kindling is little branches no thicker around than this." He held up his hand and made a circle with his first finger and thumb. "We need them to start the fire."

(4) Jake measured the circumference of the branches by wrapping his first finger and thumb around each one. If the thumb and finger touched, he put it in the pile. If his finger and thumb could not touch, he left it on the tree. After he had collected an armful, Jake brought the pile of branches to his father.

(5) His father was crumpling newspaper and arranging it around the cement circle that held up an iron grill. The wood was dry, brown, and old, but not rotten.

(6) "Perfect kindling, Jake," said his father. "Good job!" He piled the kindling on top of the newspapers and lit a match. The flames crept up the corners and edges of the paper and curled around the sticks. Soon, the flames were flickering, and Jake's father put on the first log.

(7) "What makes fire burn?" asked Jake, as he set out plates and cups on the picnic table for dinner.

(8) "Three things," said his father. "I'll give you a hint. You are breathing one of them right now."

(9) "Smoke?" asked Jake, coughing.

(10) "Oxygen," said Jake's father, laughing. "The wood we're using is another. Wood is fuel, paper is fuel, and gasoline is fuel. Anything that can burn is fuel. Finally, you need high heat, called the kindling temperature, so the fuel will catch fire and make flames."

(11) "How hot does the kindling temperature have to be?" asked Jake.

(12) "It's different for different kinds of fuel," said Jake's father. "For wood it is about 500°F (260°C). Some fuels need a higher kindling temperature, and some need a lower temperature."

(13) Jake looked down at the fire. The flames crept around the log and started to catch on to the bark. The flames flickered around the iron bars, but the bars did not burn. "Why doesn't the iron in the grill burn?" asked Jake.

(14) "It's fireproof," said Jake's father. "Oxygen cannot mix with it, so it cannot burn. It is the same with stone or brick."

(15) "It's a good thing," said Jake, as he unwrapped the hotdogs. "Or we would have to order out for pizza!"

Refer to the passage "Fire Needs Fuel and More to Burn" to answer questions 7-12.

7. Which of the following is most likely true about Jake?

a. Jake has never been in the woods before.
b. Jake is not very interested in science.
c. Jake has never made a fire before.
d. Jake is uncomfortable being in the woods.

8. Which sentence from the passage shows that Jake is a good helper?

a. "Why doesn't the iron in the grill burn?" asked Jake.
b. Soon, the flames were flickering, and Jake's father put on the first log.
c. After he had collected an armful, Jake brought the pile of branches to his father.
d. His father was crumpling newspaper and arranging it around the cement circle that held up an iron grill.

9. Which of the following describes the relationship between Jake and his dad?

a. Jake's dad encourages him and helps him learn.
b. Jake's dad gets tired of Jake's questions quickly.
c. Jake's dad does not think Jake is able to help him.
d. Jake and his dad do not have similar hobbies.

10. As Jake and his dad continue their camping trip, which event is most likely to happen?

a. Jake's dad will decide that they need to move out of their home in the city.
b. Jake will ask his dad more questions about the things they do and see.
c. Jake will gather firewood as he and his dad hike through the woods.
d. Jake will ask if they can have pizza instead of hot dogs for dinner the next night.

11. Which of the following pieces of dialogue from Jake's father supports the theme listed below?

There is always something new to learn about the world around you.

a. "Boy! You've been living in the city too long, Jake!" answered Jake's father.
b. "I'll give you a hint. You are breathing one of them right now."
c. "Perfect kindling, Jake," said his father. "Good job!"
d. "Kindling is little branches no thicker around than this."

12. In paragraph 1, the author describes a tree with "branches sticking out like a porcupine's quills." What is the purpose of this simile?

a. To help the reader understand what kindling is
b. To show the reader why Jake dislikes camping
c. To remind the reader that the woods can be dangerous
d. To help the reader imagine what the tree looks like

Ann Richards: The First Woman Governor of Texas

(1) Born Dorothy Ann Willis in 1933, Governor Ann Richards did not start out in politics. She taught social studies and history at Fulmore Junior High School in Austin, Texas. Then, she got married and stopped teaching to raise her family. While at home, Governor Richards volunteered for political campaigns and causes. She worked especially hard to make sure people were treated and paid fairly.

(2) In 1976, Governor Richards successfully campaigned to become the Travis County Commissioner. Six years later, she was elected Texas State Treasurer. She was the first woman to be elected to a statewide office in Texas in 50 years. She stayed in that office until 1990, when she was elected governor of Texas.

(3) As governor, Richards worked hard to make the state government work better. She asked that the records and budgets of every state agency be looked at carefully. This process is called an *audit*. She changed the way decisions were made for schools by giving parents and teachers more power to make important decisions. She arranged for more education programs at prisons so that prisoners would have more chances to improve themselves.

(4) Governor Richards worked to give many different kinds of people a chance to participate in the state government. Governor Richards served one term as governor. She lost in 1994 to George W. Bush, who later became president of the United States.

(5) Governor Richards was famous for having a great sense of humor and not being afraid to make fun of herself. She once joked about her hair being heavily styled by saying, "Neither snow nor rain can move my hair." To show that women were just as capable as men, she once said about a famous dancing couple that "Ginger Rogers did everything that Fred Astaire did. She just did it backwards and in high heels." Governor Richards kept working to make peoples' lives better, even after she left politics.

A Helping Hand

(1) Every person's life is affected by his or her community. This is why it is important for all of us to find ways to serve the people around us. We all have skills and talents we can use to help others around us. However, it can be difficult to find ways to help a whole community. It would be easy to give up and stop there, but there is a better way. One easy way people can start helping their communities is to just start with their own street. People should start small and help others in their neighborhoods, or even just their next-door neighbors.

(2) There may be things just outside a person's house that he or she can help with. There are opportunities to help everywhere. For example, any trash along the street can be easily picked up using gloves and trash bags. Picking up trash will keep the street clean and prevent pets and small children from playing with dirty trash. Another way people can help their neighbors is to keep an eye out for loose pets. It may be dangerous to approach an unfamiliar animal. However, telling neighbors when their pets are loose is helpful and prevents pets from getting lost. These small tasks can make a big difference, and they take little effort.

(3) One of the best ways for people to help their neighbors is to ask them what they need help doing. Elderly or injured neighbors may have trouble doing things like watering plants, taking a pet for a walk, or cleaning. Helping a neighbor do things like this can make a big difference to him or her. Sometimes, when neighbors are sick, injured, or recovering from something, they will not be able to make meals for themselves. In these cases, people can send homemade or store-bought meals to their neighbors. Both of these options allow people to help their neighbors with specific problems. These actions allow people to serve their neighbors, get to know their neighbors better, and let their neighbors know that they care for them.

(4) People can also help their neighbors by giving them opportunities to serve the community. An event like a garage sale or a bake sale will allow everyone on the street to donate items or food. These items can be sold, and the money earned from the sale can be used for good causes. For example, the money could be donated to a local charity. By organizing these events, people can bring their neighbors together and help them easily serve the community around them.

(5) When people start small, they can still make a big difference. Even things that are easy for us to do may mean a lot to the people that we help. When we start by helping the people around us, we can serve them, inspire them to help others, and help them see ways that they can help the community. The smallest service or act of kindness can lead to a bigger benefit to the community.

Refer to the passage "Ann Richards: The First Woman Governor of Texas" to answer questions 13-15.

13. This question has two parts. After you answer Part A, answer Part B:

Part A: What is paragraph 3 mostly about?

a. Gov. Richards's humor
b. Gov. Richards's life before politics
c. Gov. Richards's first job in politics
d. Gov. Richards's achievements as governor

Part B: Which sentence supports the answer to Part A?

a. She changed the way decisions were made for schools by giving parents and teachers living and working in the district more power to make important decisions.
b. Gov. Richards served one term as governor.
c. She stayed in that office until 1990, when she was elected governor of Texas.
d. To show that women were just as capable as men, she once said about a famous dancing couple that "Ginger Rogers did everything that Fred Astaire did. She just did it backwards and in high heels."

14. Which word below has the same meaning as *styled*, as it is used in paragraph 5?

a. Method
b. Fixed
c. Approach
d. Grown

15. Which of the following gives the best summary of paragraphs 3 and 4?

a. Anne Richards had other jobs, such as being a teacher and a mother, before she became the governor of Texas.
b. During her term as governor, Anne Richards worked to make sure that the Texas government did its best to help Texas citizens.
c. Anne Richards spent her time as governor making sure that no part of the Texas government was spending money unwisely.
d. Anne Richards was only the governor of Texas for one term, since George Bush became the governor 4 years after she had.

Refer to the passage "A Helping Hand" to answer questions 16-21.

16.Which of the following is the author's main argument in this passage?

a. A person's neighbors probably need more help than others in the community.
b. It is too hard for a person to help the whole community, so people should wait for others to help.
c. Every person should do his or her part to help, and a great place to start is to help neighbors.
d. Helping in small ways is more beneficial than helping in big ways.

17. Which of the following statements from the passage is an opinion?

a. However, it can be difficult to find ways to help a whole community.
b. There may be things just outside a person's house that he or she can help with.
c. Both of these options allow people to help their neighbors with specific problems.
d. Even things that are easy for us to do may mean a lot to the people that we help.

18. Which of the following actions would the author of this passage most likely suggest?

a. Organizing a pep rally to support the high school football team
b. Putting up signs around town to support someone running for president
c. Giving a presentation about the effects of littering to everyone in the town
d. Helping someone in the neighborhood pull up weeds

19. Which sentence from the passage supports the idea that helping your neighbors can be easy?

a. Every person's life is affected by his or her community.
b. These small tasks can make a big difference, and they take little effort.
c. Both of these options allow people to help their neighbors with specific problems.
d. These items can be sold, and the money earned from the sale can be used for good causes.

20. Who was this passage most likely written for? Select all that apply.

a. People who want to run for mayor
b. People who enjoy going to garage sales
c. People who do not think they need to help others
d. People looking for fun things to do around town
e. People who want to volunteer but do not know how

21. In paragraph 2, the author includes the following sentence:

There are opportunities to help everywhere.

This sentence is a hyperbole. What effect does this hyperbole have in the passage?

a. It shows that there are many different ways to help others.
b. It suggests that helping the entire community is actually easy.
c. It reveals that there are too many ways for one person to help.
d. It points out that plants and animals need help, too.

Refer to the passages "Ann Richards: The First Woman Governor of Texas" and "A Helping Hand" to answer questions 22-24.

22. Which of the following shows a difference between the message in "A Helping Hand" and the way Anne Richards helped the people of Texas?

a. "A Helping Hand" talks about helping the whole community. Anne Richards only helped a few people.
b. "A Helping Hand" talks about helping neighbors. Anne Richards helped people as a member of the state government.
c. "A Helping Hand" encourages people to participate in local government. Anne Richards was not interested in working in the government.
d. "A Helping Hand" talks about helping people in different ways. Anne Richards only helped people by improving education.

23. Which of the following statements is supported by both "Anne Richards: The First Female Governor of Texas" and "A Helping Hand"?

a. Starting small can make a big difference.
b. The state government should aim to help people.
c. Doing your part to help can benefit many people.
d. Helping people can help you get to know them.

24. Which of the following is likely a similarity between Anne Richards and the author of "A Helping Hand"?

a. They both worked in the government at some point.
b. They both have elderly neighbors who need help.
c. They both think it is important to look out for others.
d. They both started out as teachers.

Extended Response

Your STAAR test will include the following instructions for your extended response question. The response prompts used here are similar to the prompts you will see on the STAAR test.

25. Read the selections "Ann Richards: The First Woman Governor of Texas" and "A Helping Hand." Based on the information in the selections, write a response to the following:

Explain whether or not citizens should do their part to help their community.

Write a well-organized argumentative essay that uses specific evidence from the selection to support your answer.

Remember to —

- clearly state your central idea
- organize your writing
- develop your ideas in detail
- use evidence from the selections in your response
- use correct spelling, capitalization, punctuation, and grammar

Manage your time carefully so that you can —

- review the selection
- plan your response
- write your response
- revise and edit your response

Revising

Natalie wrote the following paper about pirates. Read the following paper and note the revisions that Natalie should make. Once you have read her paper, answer the questions that follow it.

Masters of the Seas

(1) Pirates have been sailing the seas for thousands of years. (2) The first recorded pirate raids occurred in 735 BC (3) During the Middle Ages, pirates lived mostly in Europe. (4) Later, pirates moved into the Caribbean, the South China Sea, and any other place with ships. (5) Many pirates took others' ships because they could not afford to buy their own.

(6) Sometimes, noblemen became pirates. (7) Some pirates were escaped slaves or criminals hiding from the law. (8) Others were gamblers, rebels, or people seeking adventure. (9) Even some women were pirates!

(10) In spite of their different backgrounds, all pirates were looking for treasure. (11) They looked for real treasure, such as gold, silver, and jewels. (12) They also looked for trading items, such as spices, cloth, and tobacco. (13) In addition, pirates looked for useful items, like tools, maps, and food. (14) Whatever items might help them later, pirates took.

(15) While many people think of pirates as part of history, there are still pirates on the seas today. (16) Modern pirates sail mostly near the coast of Africa, and they attack tanker ships and merchant ships. (17) Instead of treasure, today, pirates ask for ransom money. (18) As long as there are ships sailing, pirates will always be around.

26. Which sentence in paragraph 1 contains unnecessary information and should be removed?

a. Sentence 1
b. Sentence 3
c. Sentence 4
d. Sentence 5

27. Which of the following sentences would be a good concluding sentence for paragraph 2?

a. However, most pirates were men.
b. Pirates from different backgrounds did not get along well.
c. Pirates could come from anywhere, and anyone could become a pirate.
d. Others were crew members who joined the pirates so they would not be captured by them.

28. Which sentence would be the best topic sentence to add at the beginning of paragraph 2?

a. There were pirates who were already wealthy before they began looking for treasure.
b. Although they all raided ships, pirates came from many different backgrounds.
c. There were many ships on the seas, especially in the 1700s and 1800s.
d. Pirates were very knowledgeable in geography, and they were all excellent sailors.

29. Sentence 14 needs to be revised. Please write a revised version of sentence 14. Write the revised sentence on the lines below.

____

____

____

Grace wrote the following paper about her trip to Florida. Read the following paper and note the revisions that Grace should make. Once you have read her paper, answer the questions that follow it.

The Glass-Bottom Boat Ride

(1) One summer, my entire family went on a vacation together. (2) We got to travel through four different states to get there. (3) Then, we got to spend a whole week playing on the beach. (4) We stayed in a house near the beach, so we could walk there whenever we wanted! (5) I loved getting to swim every day, but my favorite part of the trip was riding on a glass-bottom boat.

(6) A glass-bottom boat is exactly what it sounds like. (7) It is a small boat. (8) The very bottom of the boat is made of metal and glass. (8.5) The glass bottom is like a window. (9) Instead of only seeing the surface of the water, you can also see into the ocean below the boat. (10) Many people, because they can look through the glass on glass-bottom boats during the ride, take trips.

(11) On a glass bottom boat, you do not have to wait for sea creatures to swim to the surface. (12) You can watch them as they are swimming underwater. (13) I got to see a lot of fish and some turtles! (14) I also got to see colorful coral and where the fish live. (15) The tour guide told us facts about the creatures and plants that we passed.

(16) My favorite fish that we saw on the boat is called an angelfish. (17) The ones we saw were blue and yellow. (18) Their yellow spots made them very easy to see in the water. (19) They did not swim very close to the boat, so I did not get to see them up close. (20) I like them best because they were more colorful than the other fish we saw. (21) I was sad when my parents said I couldn't get one to have as a pet.

(22) I will always remember our trip on the glass-bottom boat. (23) I will ask my parents if there is a glass-bottom boat tour close to our home. (24) It was so exciting to watch all of the fish swimming around and learn about them. (25) The next time I go on one, I would want to go farther out into the ocean.

30. Which of the following sentences would be best to add after sentence 12?

a. Dolphins swim near the surface and underwater, so you could see them on any boat.
b. Animals like sharks and octopi live in deeper water, so we didn't see any of those.
c. The boat may scare some animals away, but there are still plenty of interesting creatures that will swim near the boat.
d. Glass-bottom boats usually have seats or walkways, so passengers don't have to stand on the glass.

31. Sentences 7 and 8 should be combined. Which of the following is the best combination of sentences 7 and 8?

a. It is a small boat with glass and metal on the very bottom.
b. It is a small, metal boat made of glass.
c. The very bottom of the boat is small and made of metal and glass.
d. It is a small boat, and the very bottom of it is made of metal and glass.

32. Sentence 10 is unclear. Which of these shows the best way to revise sentence 10?

a. Many people take trips on glass-bottom boats because they can look through the glass during the ride.
b. Many people can look through the glass during the ride because they take trips on glass-bottom boats.
c. On glass-bottom boats, many people take trips because they can look through the glass during the ride.
d. They can look through the glass-bottom boats during the ride because many people take trips.

33. Which of the following sentences could replace sentence 21 as a concluding sentence for paragraph 4?

a. The tour guide told us some facts about them, and I was excited to learn even more later.
b. We also saw some scary animals in the water, like eels and snakes.
c. Angelfish also live in other parts of the world.
d. Their bright colors made them more colorful than the brown and gray fish.

Editing

Grant is writing an essay about painting. Read the first two paragraphs of Grant's essay and look for errors that he needs to correct. Once you have read the paragraphs, answer the questions that follow them.

The Art of Painting

(1) Paintings are one of the most popular types of art. (2) In fact, many art exhibits only include paintings. (3) A lot of paintings may look similar because they have the same subjects. (4) However, a closer look will show the differences between them. (5) Painters can use different tools, methods, and styles to make them art unique.

(6) A paint brush is the most common painting tool, but this is not the only one artists use. (7) Several of the other tools are made of metal. (8) One example is a painting spatula. (9) A painting spatula have a flat piece of metal that is shaped like a diamond. (10) Painting spatulas let painters add shapes to their paintings that are difficult to make with brushes. (11) Another tool painters can use is a sponge. (12) A painter can dip a sponge in paint and then add the paint to the canvas. (13) These are only a few of the many tools painters use to add details and effects to their art.

34. Choose the word that should replace them in sentence 5.

Painters can use different tools, methods, and styles to make ________ art unique.

they're
theirs
their
there

35. Which change would correct the mistake in sentence 6?

a. Change *paint brush* to *paintbrush.*
b. Remove the comma after *tool.*
c. Change *this* to *these.*
d. Change *artists* to *artist's.*

36. Which change would correct the mistake in sentence 9?

a. Change *painting spatula* to *Painting Spatula.*
b. Change *have* to *has.*
c. Change *piece* to *pece.*
d. Add a comma after *shaped.*

37. Which change needs to be made to sentence 11?

a. Change *Another* to *an other.*
b. Change *can* to *will.*
c. Change *use* to *uses.*
d. No *change* is *needed.*

Xavier is writing an essay about butterflies. Read the first two paragraphs of Xavier's essay and look for errors that he needs to correct. Once you have read the paragraphs, answer the questions that follow them.

The Life Cycle of Butterflies

(1) Spotting butterflies is one of the moast exciting parts of spring. (2) In the spring, butterflies will emerge from their chrysalises. (3) In the summer, they will lay eggs, and the caterpillars in those eggs will later become new butterflies. (4) However, they must go through a few other stages before they become butterflies. (5) First, the tiny caterpillars will hatch, and then they will emerged from the eggs. (6) They'll crawl around and eat so that they can grow. (7) After a few weeks, they will have grown much bigger.

(8) At this time, a caterpillar will find a strong structure, like a branch, and hang from it. (9) The caterpillar will form a chrysalis, which is a casing that covers the whole caterpillar and protects it as it turns into a butterfly. (10) The caterpillars whole body will change while it is in the chrysalis. (11) It will develop wings, different legs, and antennae. (12) Then, the chrysalis will open, but the butterfly will not be completely ready to fly yet. (13) The butterfly will wait while its wings finish developing. (14) Then, it will take off and fly by flower to flower until it is ready to lay eggs and start the cycle again.

38. Which change would correct the mistake in sentence 1?

a. Change *spotting* to *spoting.*
b. Change *moast* to *most.*
c. Change *of* to *to.*
d. Change *spring* to *Spring.*

39. Which change needs to be made to sentence 5?

a. Add a comma before *from.*
b. Change *emerged* to *emerge.*
c. Change *eggs* to *egg's.*
d. No change is needed.

40. Which change would correct the mistake in sentence 10?

a. Change *caterpillars* to *caterpillar's.*
b. Change *changes* to *changed.*
c. Change *is* to *are.*
d. Change *in* to *on.*

41. Which change would correct the mistake in sentence 14?

a. Change *take* to *took.*
b. Change *by* to *from.*
c. Change *is* to *are.*
d. Change *cycle* to *cycles.*

Answer Key and Explanations for Test #2

Reading

1. D: TEKS Standard (3.10)(A)

Each paragraph in this passage focuses on telling the reader about Mercury, so choice D is correct. There are eight planets in the solar system, but only three are mentioned in the passage, so choice B is incorrect. The number of days in a year is part of a supporting detail in the passage. However, it is not the central idea, so choice B is incorrect. The Sun is mentioned multiple times in this passage. However, the passage is about Mercury, not the Sun, making choice C incorrect.

2. C: TEKS Standard (3.3)(D)

Paragraph 1 says that Mercury is barren and that there is nothing but soil on the surface. This includes plants. The author is trying to show the reader that there is no life on the planet. In this sentence, the word *barren* is used as a synonym for *lifeless,* making choice C correct. Paragraph 1 also says that Mercury has many craters. This means that Mercury is not smooth, so choice B is incorrect. The fact that Mercury's surface is covered in soil shows that its surface is not blue in color. This shows that *barren* does not mean *blue*, so choice A is incorrect. Mercury is a small planet, and there are no words in the passage that suggest that it is very big. This means that *barren* cannot mean *gigantic*, so choice D is incorrect.

3. B: TEKS Standard (3.3)(B)

The passage says that the name *Mercury* came from Ancient Rome and that Ancient Rome existed about 24 centuries ago. A century is 100 years, so Ancient Rome existed 2,400 years ago. However, Rome still exists today. This means that the phrase "Ancient Rome" is talking about things that happened in Rome a very long time ago, meaning choice B is the correct answer. The passage does not talk about how far away Rome is, so choice A is incorrect. Rome was and is a real place, so choice D is incorrect. *Recent* means something happened or existed not long ago. This has a meaning that is the opposite of the explanation given in the passage, so choice C is incorrect.

4. TEKS Standard (3.6)(H)

The passage says that Mercury is closer to the Sun than Earth is. The Sun is extremely hot. Things that are closer to a heat source are usually hotter than things that are farther away from it. Mercury is much hotter than Earth because Mercury is closer to the Sun than Earth is.

5. B: TEKS Standard (3.6)(G)

The introductory sentence of paragraph 4 says that humans will never live on Mercury. The concluding sentence also says this. The supporting details in paragraph 4 explain why people cannot live on Mercury's surface. This means that choice B is correct. The paragraph does not explain why there are extreme temperatures on Mercury, so choice C is incorrect. Paragraph 3 explains that a day on Mercury is as long as about 58 days on Earth. This means that choice A is incorrect. The passage does not talk about seasons on Mercury, so choice D is incorrect.

6. C: TEKS Standard (3.10)(C)

This diagram shows the reader what order the planets are in and how far each one is from the Sun. This means that the diagram shows the reader how close Mercury is to the Sun, so choice C is correct. This picture does not help the reader understand how Mercury was discovered, so choice A is incorrect. The temperatures on Mercury and the way it got its name are related to how close it is to the Sun. However, the diagram's main purpose is to help the reader see how close Mercury is to the Sun, so choices B and D are incorrect.

7. C: TEKS Standard (3.6)(F)

Jake asks his father what kindling wood is, and his father explains that they need it for the fire. He also tells Jake what to look for when he is gathering kindling wood. This shows that Jake is not very familiar with how to make a fire, so choice C is the best choice. The passage does not show that Jake is unfamiliar with the woods, so choice A is incorrect. Jake asks many questions about fire and how it works. This shows that he may be interested in science, so choice B is wrong. Jake gathers kindling wood on his own and does not do anything that makes him seem nervous or upset. This means that choice D is incorrect.

8. C: TEKS Standard (3.7)(C)

The sentence in choice C shows that Jake collected branches for the fire his dad was going to build. This sentence also says that he collected an armful of branches. Instead of only getting a few branches, Jake put in the effort to collect many branches. This shows that he is a good helper, so choice C is correct. The sentence in choice A shows Jake asking a question. Jake only asks this question because he is curious. He does not ask it so that he can help his dad, so choice A is incorrect. Choices B and D describe Jake's father's actions, not Jake's. Choices B and D are incorrect.

9. A: TEKS Standard (3.8)(B)

Jake asks his father several questions, and his father answers them happily. He also allows Jake to help him gather kindling instead of telling Jake to wait while he does it. Jake's father helps him learn, so choice A is correct. Jake's dad does not tell Jake to stop asking questions, nor does he act like he wants Jake to stop. Choice B is incorrect. Jake's father tells Jake to help him gather kindling for the fire, so choice C is incorrect. The passage does not mention Jake's hobbies or his dad's hobbies. While Jake's dad has probably been camping more times than Jake has, the passage does not say that camping is one of his hobbies. This makes choice D incorrect.

10. B: TEKS Standard (3.6)(C)

Jake shows that he is curious about the fire and how it works by asking questions. Jake is likely to be curious about more of the things he and his dad will see, and he will probably ask more questions. Choice B is correct. Jake's dad tells Jake that he has been living in the city for too long. When he says this, he is picking on Jake for not knowing what kindling wood is. This does not mean that Jake's dad actually wants to move from the city, so choice A is incorrect. Jake only gathered firewood because his dad asked him to gather it. Jake will probably not start gathering more wood unless they prepare to build another fire, so choice C is incorrect. Jake says they would have to order pizza if they couldn't cook the hot dogs. This does not mean that Jake would rather eat pizza, so choice D is incorrect.

11. B: TEKS Standard (3.8)(A)

Jake's father's statement in choice B shows that he is going to teach Jake about something that is around them every day. This shows that there is something Jake can learn about something that is part of the world around him. Choice B is correct. In choices A and C, Jake's dad does not teach Jake anything or mention learning, making them incorrect. In choice D, Jake's father tells him what kind of branches to gather for kindling. While Jake learns something from this, what he learns does not tell him something about the world around him, so choice D is incorrect.

12. D: TEKS Standard (3.10)(D)

This simile tells the reader that the branches are thin and sticking out in all directions, like a porcupine's quills. This tells the reader what the tree looks like, so choice D is correct. This description does not give the reader more information about what kindling is, so choice A is incorrect. Choice B is incorrect because this simile describes the tree, not Jake's opinion about camping. The tree has branches that are sticking out, but it is not dangerous. The simile does not show that the tree or the woods are dangerous, so choice C is incorrect.

13. TEKS Standard (3.6)(G)

Part A: D: Paragraph 3 describes some of the actions Governor Richards took while she was the governor of Texas. Choice D is the best description of the main idea of this paragraph. Governor Richards's sense of humor is described in paragraph 5, so choice A is incorrect. Governor Richards's life before she became a politician is summarized in paragraph 1, so choice B is incorrect. Governor Richards's first job in politics is discussed in paragraph 2, so choice C is incorrect.

Part B: A: Choice A describes one of the things Governor Richards accomplished during her term as governor. This sentence can be found in paragraph 3 of the passage and is a supporting detail related to the topic of Governor Richards's achievements as governor. Choice A is correct. Choices B and C are incorrect because, though they are facts about Governor Richards's time as governor, they do not show what she accomplished. Choice D is a sentence from paragraph 5, so it is incorrect.

14. B: TEKS Standard (3.3)(C)

The word *styled* is used as a verb. It is also used to show that Governor Richards spent time making sure her hair looked the way she wanted it to. The word *fix* is a verb that can mean to improve or correct something. *Fixed* could be used in place of *styled* in paragraph 5, so choice B is correct. *Method* is a noun, so it does not have the same meaning as *styled* in paragraph 5, making choice A incorrect. *Approach* means to go near something or attempt to do something. These definitions do not match the meaning of *styled*, so choice C is incorrect. The word *styled* is used to show what Governor Richards did to her hair, not how long it had grown, making Choice D incorrect.

15. B: TEKS Standard (3.7)(D)

Paragraphs 3 and 4 describe what Governor Richards aimed to do while she was governor. Overall, her goal was to make changes that would help the citizens of Texas. This matches the summary in choice B, so it is the correct answer. Choice A summarizes information given in paragraph 1, so it is incorrect. Choice C summarizes one detail from paragraph 3. This does not explain the meaning of paragraphs 3 and 4, so choice C is incorrect. Choice D summarizes a detail from paragraph 4. It also does not summarize all of the information in the two paragraphs, so choice D is incorrect.

16. C: TEKS Standard (3.9)(Ei)

The passage says that every person should try to help the people in his or her community. The passage also says that finding ways to help everyone can be a challenge. The main argument is that everyone should start by helping his or her neighbors because that is a simple way to start helping the community. This means that choice C is correct. The passage does not say which people in a community need the most help, so choice A is incorrect. The passage also does not say that small actions are more helpful than big actions. This means choice D is incorrect. Choice B is incorrect because the passage recommends starting small. It does not recommend waiting for others to help.

17. A: TEKS Standard (3.9)(Eii)

There are few things that every person will agree are difficult. This means that whether something is difficult or easy is an opinion. Choice A states an opinion, so it is correct. Choice B says there may be opportunities to help just outside a person's house. This is a fact, so choice B is incorrect. Choice C says that sending store-bought or homemade food to neighbors who need it is a way that someone can help with a specific problem. This is a fact because it is always true, so choice C is incorrect. Choice D says that there are easy actions that can make a difference to someone else. This is always true, so it is a fact. Choice D is incorrect.

18. D: TEKS Standard (3.6)(F)

Helping someone remove weeds is an easy and quick way to help a neighbor. This is the type of action the author wants people to take, so choice D is correct. Organizing a pep rally may be helpful for members of the football team, but this is not a simple way that a person can help his or her neighbors, making choice A incorrect. Choice B is incorrect because persuading people to vote for a person running for president is not an easy way to help people nearby. Persuading people not to litter may help reduce litter and pollution in a town or city. However, this takes a lot of time and effort, so choice C is incorrect.

19. B: TEKS Standard (3.7)(C)

Choice B says that small tasks can take little effort. This means that they can be easy, so choice B is correct. Choice A does not mention helping neighbors, so it is incorrect. Choice C talks about helping neighbors, but it does not say that helping them is easy, so it is incorrect. Choice D gives an example of a way to help others. However, it does not say that this is an easy action to take, so choice D is incorrect.

20. C, E: TEKS Standard (3.9)(Eiii)

This passage is meant to persuade people to look for ways to help others around them. This passage is written to persuade people who do not want to help their communities to find ways to help. It is also written to persuade people who do not know how to start helping to start by helping their neighbors. This means choices C and E are correct. This passage is not meant for people who want to run for mayor. Running for mayor is a good way to help a lot of people in a community. These people do not need to be persuaded to help their communities, so choice A is incorrect. This passage mentions garage sales as a way to help others, but it is not about garage sales, so choice B is incorrect. This passage is not meant to help people find fun things to do in their city or town, so choice D is incorrect.

21. A: TEKS Standard (3.10)(G)

This statement is a hyperbole, which means that it is an exaggeration. The author uses this exaggeration to suggest that there is a large number of ways that people can help others. This means that choice A is correct. The statement does not say that the number of opportunities makes it easy to help the whole community. It also does not say that there are too many ways to help others. It simply means that finding an opportunity to help should be easy, so choices B and C are incorrect. This statement does not describe who or what these opportunities will help, so choice D is incorrect.

22. B: TEKS Standard (3.6)(E)

The author's message in "A Helping Hand" is that people should look for opportunities to help their neighbors. "Anne Richards: The First Female Governor of Texas" describes Anne Richards's career and what she did during her term as governor. This makes choice B correct. Since Anne Richards was the governor of Texas, she worked in the government and helped people throughout the state. This means choices A and C are incorrect. Anne Richards did more than just improve education, so choice D is incorrect.

23. C: TEKS Standard (3.6)(E)

The author of "A Helping Hand" claims that looking for ways to help your neighbors can allow you to help many people. In "Anne Richards: The First Female Governor of Texas," the author shows how Anne Richards used her time as governor to help many people. This means that choice C is correct. "Anne Richards: The First Female Governor of Texas" is about how Anne Richards helped by making changes that impacted all of Texas. This is not an example of starting small, so choice A is incorrect. The government is not mentioned in "A Helping Hand," so choice B is incorrect. Whether or not Anne Richards was able to get to know the people she helped was not mentioned in "Anne Richards: The First Female Governor of Texas." This means choice D is incorrect.

24. C: TEKS Standard (3.6)(E)

The author of "A Helping Hand" wants to persuade people to help and look out for others. Anne Richards worked to make changes that would help people. She also wanted to create opportunities for people who did not always have them. This means that choice C is correct. There are no details in "A Helping Hand" that show what jobs the author has had, so choices A and D are incorrect. The passage "Anne Richards: The First Female Governor of Texas" does not talk about Anne Richards's neighbors, so choice B is incorrect.

Extended Response

25. TEKS Standard (3.12)(C)

Please use the rubric below to make sure your response meets these common criteria. Try to have a friend or family member grade your response for you or take a break after writing your response and return to grade it yourself with fresh eyes.

Below is an excerpt of the STAAR Grades 3-5 Argumentative/Opinion Writing Rubric.

Score Point	Development and Organization of Ideas
3	• **Argument/opinion is clear and fully developed** The argument/opinion is clearly identifiable. The focus is consistent throughout, creating a response that is unified and easy to follow. • **Organization is effective** A purposeful structure that includes an effective introduction and conclusion is evident. The organizational structure is appropriate and effectively supports the development of the argument/opinion. The sentences, paragraphs, or ideas are logically connected in purposeful and highly effective ways. • **Evidence is specific, well chosen, and relevant** The response includes relevant text-based evidence that is clearly explained and consistently supports and develops the argument/opinion. For pairs in grades 3-5, evidence is drawn from at least one text. The response reflects a thorough understanding of the writing purpose. • **Expression of ideas is clear and effective** The writer's word choice is specific, purposeful, and enhances the response. Almost all sentences and phrases are effectively crafted to convey the writer's ideas and contribute to the overall quality of the response and the clarity of the message.

Score Point	Conventions
2	Student writing demonstrates **consistent command** of grade-level-appropriate conventions, including correct: • sentence construction • punctuation • capitalization • grammar • spelling The response has few errors, but those errors do not impact the clarity of the writing.

Revising

26. D: TEKS Standard (3.11)(Bii)

Paragraph 1 is about the history of pirates. The paragraph includes supporting details that explain how long pirates have been around. The supporting details also tell the reader where pirates lived and sailed. These details all work together to help the reader understand pirates' history. However, sentence 5 gives a reason that pirates stole ships. This sentence is off topic and unrelated to the other information in the paragraph, so choice D is correct. Sentence 1 tells how long pirates have existed. This sentence is on topic, so choice A is incorrect. Sentences 3 and 4 explain which areas pirates often lived in, so they are also on topic, making choices B and C incorrect.

27. C: TEKS Standard (3.11)(Bi)

A concluding sentence should be related to the main point of the paragraph. Choice C is related to the main idea of the paragraph, which is that pirates came from different places and backgrounds, so it is correct. Choice A is incorrect because it is only related to the last sentence in the paragraph. Choice B is incorrect because, even though it mentions that pirates came from different backgrounds, it talks about a new idea. The rest of the paragraph does not talk about how well pirates got along with each other. Choice D is incorrect because it talks about crew members who tried to avoid being captured. This topic is not related to the rest of the paragraph.

28. B: TEKS Standard (3.11)(Bi)

The sentences in paragraph 2 describe how many pirates lived before becoming pirates. These sentences say that some pirates had been noblemen, criminals, rebels, or adventurers. The topic sentence should show the reader what the paragraph is about. Using choice B as the topic sentence would let the reader know that the paragraph talks about how pirates came from different lifestyles. Choice B is correct. Choice A only talks about pirates who were wealthy before becoming pirates, so it is incorrect. Choice C would tell the reader that the paragraph is about different pirate ships, so it is also incorrect. Choice D is incorrect because it would make it seem like the rest of the paragraph is mainly about the skills that pirates had.

29. TEKS Standard (3.11)(C)

The revised sentence should be similar to the following sentence: Pirates took whatever items might help them later. A correctly revised sentence may be slightly different from this sentence. It should be a complete sentence that is easy to understand and uses proper grammar and spelling. The original sentence is unclear because it communicates information in an order that may be unclear or difficult to understand.

30. C: TEKS Standard (3.11)(Bii)

The topic sentence of paragraph 3 shows that the paragraph's main idea is that you can see animals underwater from a glass-bottom boat. Choice C is a supporting detail that is related to this main idea. Choice A is a supporting detail, but it is off topic because it is about being able to see dolphins from any type of boat. Choice B is also off topic, because it is about animals that you cannot see from a glass-bottom boat. Choice D is incorrect because it is not related to the main idea of this paragraph at all. Choice D is about walkways and seats on glass-bottom boats, not the animals you can see from a glass-bottom boat.

31. D: TEKS Standard (3.11)(C)

Choice D includes the details that are given in both sentence 7 and sentence 8, it makes sense, and it is grammatically correct. Choice A is incorrect because it changes the meaning of the information from the original sentences. Choice A says that there is glass and metal on the very bottom of the boat. This does not mean the same thing as saying that the very bottom of the boat is made of glass and metal. Choice B is incorrect because it does not make sense. It says that the whole boat is made of metal and that the whole boat is made of glass, which is not possible. Choice C is incorrect because it also changes the meaning of the original sentences. Choice C says that the very bottom of the boat is small. The original sentences say that the entire boat is small.

32. A: TEKS Standard (3.11)(C)

Sentence 10 is unclear because it states ideas in an order that is difficult to understand. Choice A states these ideas in an order that is clear. The sentence in choice A states that people want to go on glass-bottom boats because they can look through the glass. Choice B is incorrect because it says that people can look through the glass because they ride on glass-bottom boats. This does not make sense. Someone could look through the glass without taking a trip on the boat. Choice C is incorrect because it is not clear. Choice D is incorrect because it states that people can look through the glass-bottom boat because many people take trips. The fact that people go on trips does not make others able to look through the glass in the boat. This sentence also does not make sense.

33. A: TEKS Standard (3.11)(Bi)

Paragraph 4 is about the author seeing angelfish during a ride on the glass-bottom boat. Choice A says that the tour guide shared some facts about angelfish and that the author planned to learn more about them after the boat ride. This could be a good concluding sentence for paragraph 4 because it wraps up the paragraph and prepares the reader for the next paragraph. Choice B is incorrect because it is off topic. It talks about animals that are not mentioned in this paragraph. Choice C is incorrect because, even though it is about angelfish, it is not related to the author's trip on the glass-bottom boat. Choice D is incorrect because it simply repeats the ideas that were stated in sentence 20.

Editing

34. their: TEKS Standard (3.11)(Dvii)

Their, *they're*, and *there* are homophones. T*hey're* is a contraction of *they* and *are*, and *there* is a pronoun that is used to represent a location. *Theirs* and *their* can both be used as adjectives that show ownership. *Theirs* is used after a verb. *Their* is used before a noun. This sentence is talking about art that is made by painters. This means that the art belongs to the painters. A possessive adjective can be used to show this. Since the blank is before the noun, the correct word to use is *their*.

35. A: TEKS Standard (3.2)(Biii)

Paintbrush is a compound word that is spelled without a space, so choice A is correct. In a compound sentence, independent clauses are joined by a comma and a coordinating conjunction. Sentence 6 is a compound sentence, so a comma is needed between *tool* and *but*. This makes choice B incorrect. *This* is a singular pronoun, and *these* is a plural pronoun. In this sentence, the pronoun replaces the singular noun *paintbrush*. *This* is the correct pronoun to use, so choice C is incorrect. *Artists* is not possessive in this sentence, so it does not need an apostrophe added to it, making choice D incorrect.

36. B: TEKS Standard (3.11)(Di)

Painting spatula is a singular noun, so it should be used with a singular verb. *Have* is a plural verb, and *has* is a singular verb. In this sentence, *has* should be used instead of *had*, so choice B is correct. A painting spatula is an object, so it is not a proper noun. *Painting spatula* does not need to be capitalized, so choice A is incorrect. The word *piece* is spelled using the vowel team *ie* and a silent *e*. It is spelled correctly in the passage, so choice C is incorrect. There is no reason to add a comma after shaped, so choice D is incorrect.

37. D: TEKS Standard (3.11)(D)

This sentence is written correctly, so choice D is correct. The word *another* is a compound word and is not written using a space. This means choice A is incorrect. Changing *can* to *will* would change the meaning of this sentence. The meaning of the sentence does not need to change, so choice B is incorrect. *Painters* is a plural noun, so it should be used with a plural verb. *Use* is a plural verb, while *uses* is singular. This means that choice C is incorrect.

38. B: TEKS Standard (3.11)(Dxi)

The word *most* is not spelled using a vowel team. The spelling used in the passage contains an extra letter, so choice B is correct. The word *spotting* is spelled using a double consonant, so it is spelled correctly in the passage. This makes choice A incorrect. Changing *of* to *to* would change the meaning of the sentence. The sentence would not make sense with this change, so choice C is incorrect. Seasons are not proper nouns, so they do not need to be capitalized, making choice D incorrect.

39. B: TEKS Standard (3.11)(Dii)

This sentence is in future tense. The verb *emerged* is only used in the past tense, so it should be changed to *emerge*. Commas are often added after prepositional phrases. They do not need to be added before prepositional phrases, so choice A is incorrect. In this sentence, *eggs* is not possessive, so it does not need an apostrophe. This means choice C is incorrect. Since *emerged* needs to be changed to *emerge*, choice D is incorrect.

40. A: TEKS Standard (3.11)(Dx)

In this sentence, *caterpillars* is a singular possessive noun. Since it is possessive, an apostrophe should be added before the *s*. This makes choice A correct. This sentence is in the future tense. *Changed* is only used in the past tense, so choice B is incorrect. Since *it* is a singular pronoun, it should be used with a singular verb. *Is* is a singular verb, and *are* is a plural verb. *Is* is the correct verb to use, so choice C is incorrect. When a caterpillar changes, it is inside its chrysalis, not on top of it. *In* is the correct preposition to use here, so choice D is incorrect.

41. B: TEKS Standard (3.11)(Dvi)

Butterflies leave one flower and then fly to another flower. *By* means that something is beside, or next to, something else. Since the butterflies land in the flowers, they are not just next to them. *By* should be changed to *from*, so choice B is correct. This sentence is in the future tense. *Took* is only used in the past tense, so choice A is incorrect. *It* is a singular pronoun, so should be used with a singular verb. *Is* is a singular verb, and *are* is a plural verb. This means choice C is incorrect. The word *the* shows that the sentence is only talking about one cycle. *Cycle* is singular, and *cycles* is plural. An *s* does not need to be added to *cycle*, so choice D is incorrect.

Practice Test #3

Reading

Bed in Summer

by Robert Louis Stevenson

In winter I get up at night
And dress by yellow candle-light.
In summer, quite the other way,
I have to go to bed by day.

I have to go to bed and see
The birds still hopping on the tree,
Or hear the grown-up people's feet
Still going past me in the street.

And does it not seem hard to you,
When all the sky is clear and blue,
And I should like so much to play,
To have to go to bed by day?

Refer to the passage "Bed in Summer" to answer questions 1-6.

1. Which line from the poem shows that the speaker wants to do something other than go to sleep?

a. And dress by yellow candle-light
b. The birds still hopping on the tree
c. And does it not seem hard to you
d. And I should like so much to play

2. Which of the following themes can be found in this poem?

a. It is not always fun to do things that are good for us.
b. The Sun never goes down during the summer.
c. Life is always easier for grown-ups.
d. Children should always go to sleep early.

3. What is the purpose of stanza 2 in this poem?

a. It shows what the speaker dreams about during the summer.
b. It shows what others are doing while the speaker is going to bed.
c. It shows why the speaker has to go to bed while the Sun is still out.
d. It shows why the speaker wants to stay up instead of going to bed.

4. How will the speaker most likely feel in the morning?

a. The speaker will be disappointed that the birds are out again.
b. The speaker will be angry that it is time to wake up.
c. The speaker will be excited to get up and play again.
d. The speaker will be glad that he or she went to bed so early.

5. What is the effect of the poet using a first-person narrator for this poem?

a. The reader knows what the grown-ups think of the narrator.
b. The reader knows what time the narrator goes to sleep
c. The reader knows the speaker's thoughts and feelings.
d. The reader knows how the narrator and the grown-ups feel.

6. How does the narrator most likely feel about the grown-ups walking in the street?

a. The narrator thinks the grown-ups walk too slow.
b. The narrator is jealous of the grown-ups.
c. The narrator is angry at the grown-ups for being awake.
d. The narrator does not want to become a grown-up.

The State Fair of Texas

Manuela wrote the following journal entry about her visit to the annual State Fair in Dallas, Texas.

October 11, 2009

(1) My father woke me up early, at 6 a.m., so we could get to the Texas State Fair in time to get a good parking spot. This was my first visit to the fair. I am eight years old, and I live near Dallas, where the fair is held every year from late September to early October. We quickly ate breakfast. Dad put his coffee in a thermos cup so he could finish it on the drive.

(2) It only took us 20 minutes to get to the fairgrounds, but we had to wait for 30 minutes to get a parking space! By the time we got into the fair, it was almost 8 a.m. We were at the fair to see my cousin Gloria with her prize goats. Gloria is four years older than I am. She lives on a farm near Austin where her family raises goats and sheep. They use the animals' milk to make cheese and the sheep's wool to make yarn. Gloria has five goats, and she was showing two of them.

(3) Gloria's goats are Nubian. They have short hair and very long, dangly ears. Gloria's two goats are named Maja and Henry. Maja, a girl, is white with black and tan spots. Henry, a boy, is mostly black with white feet and a white spot on his throat.

(4) Gloria was judged on how her goats looked. Gloria had washed and brushed both goats, so they had very shiny coats. The goats were not very tall. Maja's head came up to my chest, and Henry was tall enough to rest his chin on my shoulder. Gloria said they were supposed to look well fed, but not fat.

(5) "No ribs showing and no belly sticking out," she had said as she walked Maja around the pen.

(6) The goats were also judged on how well they behaved in front of the judges. Gloria got points if the goats followed her and did everything she told them to do. She lost points if the goats did not follow her or if they ran away. Gloria said that last year, her friend's goat got only halfway around the ring before a whistle scared him and he ran back to the gate.

(7) Finally, it was time for Gloria to show her goats. She brought out Maja first. Maja was wearing a harness with a leash attached to it. Maja followed Gloria very quietly until they reached the judge's table. Then, Maja began to bleat. At first, she bleated softly, but then she got louder. By the time Gloria brought her back to the gate, Maja was bleating very loudly.

(8) I wondered if the judges took away points if the goat was noisy while it was being shown. Henry was much better. He did everything Gloria told him to do without making a sound. I thought for sure Henry would get a prize.

(9) After Gloria was finished, we waited for the judges to announce the prizes. We were so surprised when Maja got second place!

(10) "I guess the judges understand Goat," joked Gloria, as she showed off her prizes. Henry only got an honorable mention.

(11) We had a great time at the fair. I learned a lesson from Maja. Sometimes fortune does favor the bold!

Do Your Best

Cast of Characters:

- Bailey: A girl in the fourth grade
- Savannah: A girl in the fourth grade
- Daniel: A boy in the fourth grade.
- Mr. Dawn: The elementary school music teacher

SCENE 1

[BAILEY'S *room.* BAILEY *and* SAVANNAH *are standing in front of* BAILEY'S *cd player. A SONG ends and* SAVANNAH *pushes a button on the cd player.*]

SAVANNAH: Well, that didn't go so great.

BAILEY: I know! I messed up so many times.

SAVANNAH: I can't believe the audition is tomorrow. It feels like we've only had a little while to practice.

BAILEY: I just want to be able to sing it perfectly just once before tomorrow.

SAVANNAH: Me too. But we've practiced a lot. All we can do now is to just try our best.

[BAILEY *nods and looks at the floor.*]

SAVANNAH: Hey, it'll be okay! I'm sure everyone else is just as nervous as we are.

BAILEY: Yeah, I guess you're right.

SCENE 2:

[*The music room at the school. Several students are sitting in rows of chairs. The door to the audition room opens, and* SAVANNAH *walks through it and sits in the chair next to* BAILEY. MR. DAWN *steps into the doorway and looks at the clipboard in his hand.*]

MR. DAWN: Okay, next up is... Daniel!

[DANIEL *gets up and follows* MR. DAWN *back through the doorway. The door closes.*]

BAILEY: Well, how did it go?

SAVANNAH: Okay, I guess. I think I still messed up a few times.

[BAILEY nods. The two girls sit in silence for a few moments.]

BAILEY: Oh man, I'm still so nervous! I don't think I can do it.

SAVANNAH: You can do it! You barely messed up in practice yesterday. Just do the best you can! I think you'll make the choir.

BAILEY: Thanks. I'm still not so sure.

[The door opens again. DANIEL walks out and sits back down. MR. DAWN steps through the doorway.]

MR. DAWN: Bailey? Your turn!

[BAILEY *stands up slowly.*]

SAVANNAH: [*Quietly.*] You'll do great! Good luck!

SCENE 3:

[*The audition room.* BAILEY *closes the door behind her and stands in front of a black curtain.* MR. DAWN *and two other teachers are sitting on the other side of the curtain. MUSIC plays.* BAILEY *opens her mouth to sing but is silent. She waits until the MUSIC ends and walks back through the door.*]

SCENE 4:

[*The music room at the elementary school, an hour later.* MR. DAWN *walks out of the audition room with a piece of paper.*]

MR. DAWN: Great job, kids! Alright, the list of students who have made the choir is on a list right here.

[MR. DAWN *puts the paper on the whiteboard. All of the students, except for* BAILEY, *walk over to look at it.* SAVANNAH *looks at the list and sits back down.*]

BAILEY: Did you make it?

SAVANNAH: Yeah, I did! I thought for sure that I messed up too many times.

[MR. DAWN *walks over to where* BAILEY *and* SAVANNAH *are sitting.*]

MR. DAWN: Bailey, what happened? Why didn't you sing?

BAILEY: I was nervous that I would mess up, and when I tried to sing, nothing happened. So, I gave up.

MR. DAWN: I see. Everyone messes up sometimes, but you shouldn't let that stop you from trying your best. But I understand stage fright and getting nervous. That still happens to me, too!

BAILEY: Really?

MR. DAWN: All of the time! But things don't usually go as bad as I think they will. When I do the very best that I can, I usually do much better than I thought I could.

BAILEY: Man, I didn't think about it that way. I wish I had tried to sing again. I'm a little disappointed in myself.

MR. DAWN: Hey, it'll be alright! There's always next year. Now you have a whole year to practice and get ready to try again.

BAILEY: You're right. Next time, even if I'm scared, I'll do the best that I can.

THE END

Refer to the passage "The State Fair of Texas" to answer questions 7-9.

7. Why was Manuela sure that Henry would get a prize instead of Maja?

a. He looked like he was healthy and well fed.
b. He was quiet while Gloria was showing him.
c. His coat was shiny and mostly one color.
d. He was almost as tall as Manuela.

8. What is the purpose of paragraph 7?

a. It lists Maja's qualities and explains why she won second place.
b. It explains what the goats are expected to do when they are being shown in the ring.
c. It describes the events that lead to the narrator's surprise at the end of the story.
d. It tells why the narrator is disappointed that Maja received a better award than Henry.

9. Which of the following correctly summarizes paragraphs 7 and 8?

a. Henry performed well and followed Gloria. Maja ran away from Gloria in the ring.
b. Both of Gloria's goats performed well. In the end, they tied for second place.
c. Maja obeys Gloria, but she begins bleating. Henry also obeys Gloria but is silent.
d. Henry is disqualified for being too noisy. Maja follows and obeys Gloria perfectly.

Refer to the passage "Do Your Best" to answer questions 10-13.

10. What does this play have in common with fables?

a. It includes talking animals.
b. It teaches a lesson.
c. It has one main character.
d. It does not have a happy ending.

11. This stage direction is used in scene 2:

[*The door opens again. DANIEL walks out and sits back down.* MR. DAWN *steps through the doorway.*]

What can the reader infer based on this stage direction?

a. Daniel also got nervous.
b. Daniel did not make the choir.
c. Daniel's audition was over.
d. Daniel forgot his music at home.

12. In scene 4, Bailey says "I'm a little disappointed in myself." What does *disappointed* mean?

a. Angry
b. Let down
c. Excited
d. Proud

13. How does the box titled "Cast of Characters" at the beginning of the passage help the reader?

a. It tells the reader what kind of costumes each character would wear.
b. It tells the reader what each character's voice should sound like.
c. It tells the reader about each character's role in the story.
d. It tells the reader about the skills that each character has.

Refer to the passages "The State Fair of Texas" and "Do Your Best" to answer questions 14-16.

14. Which of the following describes one similarity between Manuela in "The State Fair of Texas" and Savannah in "Do Your Best"?

a. Manuela did not sing during her audition. Savannah also did not sing during her audition.
b. Manuela showed goats in front of a group of judges. Savannah sang for a group of judges.
c. Manuela was surprised that Maja got second place. Savannah was surprised she made the choir.
d. Manuela's goat got second place. Savannah's goat only received an honorable mention.

15. What is one difference between Gloria in "The State Fair of Texas" and Bailey in "Do Your Best"?

a. Gloria was auditioning to be in the choir. Bailey was showing goats at the fair.
b. Gloria was not rewarded for her hard work. Bailey was rewarded for her hard work.
c. Gloria did not have to prepare her goats. Bailey did have to prepare for the audition.
d. Gloria did not give up when Maja began bleating. Bailey gave up during her audition.

16. Which of the following ideas is shown in both "The State Fair of Texas" and "Do Your Best"?

a. Things may turn out better than you expect them to.
b. There are always second chances.
c. Practice does not always make perfect.
d. It is normal to have stage fright.

Linda Richards: Medical Pioneer

(1) There are people whose job is to take care of us while we're being treated by doctors. These people are called nurses, and they have helped hundreds of millions of Americans feel better and get well faster over the years. All of us should be grateful for nurses because nearly all of us have been helped by a nurse at one time or another, and we all have several family members who have been brought back to health thanks to the efforts of nurses. Linda Richards is one of the pioneers of modern nursing.

(2) Linda Richards was born in West Potsdam, New York, in 1841. Her father was a preacher, and he wanted Linda to become a missionary when she grew up. However, her father died when she was only four years old. Then, her mother became very sick, and Linda spent years taking care of her mother. Linda's mother died when Linda was fourteen. Linda had enjoyed taking care of her mother, and Linda decided that she was going to become a nurse, not a missionary.

(3) Linda Richards was not the first nurse in the world by any stretch of the imagination. Nurses have been around for centuries, but, until recently, nursing was a lot different than it is today. Back in the old days, most nurses were not well educated. Some of them couldn't read or write, and they knew little about medicine or health. They mostly did things to make patients feel more comfortable, such as give them a drink of water, help them go to the bathroom, or wipe their foreheads with a wet rag. These tasks are very important, but there is a lot more a nurse needs to know and do to help people get well. Linda Richards understood that, and she helped change nursing into the modern profession it is today.

(4) After helping a local doctor for a while, she took a nursing job at a hospital in Boston, but it was an awful experience. There was no training, and nurses were expected to work from 6 in the morning to 9:30 at night. They also had to sleep at the hospital, near their patients. They would have to get up every time a patient called them. This was very hard on nurses, and many of them quit, including Linda. She soon became a student in the first class ever held at America's very first nursing school. After she graduated, she became a supervisor at Bellevue Hospital in New York City. While she worked there, she invented a way of keeping records for each patient. At the time, most hospitals did not keep very good track of their patients and their health. However, Linda Richards changed all of that. Before long, all hospitals in America were keeping patient records.

(5) Linda Richards didn't stop there. She kept getting more education for herself. She even went to England to study with Florence Nightingale, one of the most famous nurses in history. After she returned to America, she began starting nursing schools across the country. At these schools, she trained people in the modern methods of nursing. Pretty soon, nurses who had an education in medicine were helping patients all over America. Linda Richards's efforts greatly improved nursing in America. Thanks to her, millions of people have lived longer and better lives.

Refer to the passage "Linda Richards: Medical Pioneer" to answer questions 17-25.

17. Which of these words has a similar meaning to *pioneer*?

a. Follower
b. Inventor
c. Traveler
d. Patient

18. Which of the definitions above matches the way that *record* is used in paragraph 4?

Record *(noun)* pronounced: reh-kord 1. a vinyl disc that can be used to play music 2. an album of songs by a band or musician 3. the best performance of a task or feat 4. a written or typed copy of information

a. Definition 1
b. Definition 2
c. Definition 3
d. Definition 4

19. What would be the best word to describe the working conditions Linda Richards experienced at her first hospital job in Boston? Select all that apply.

a. Pleasant
b. Enjoyable
c. Harsh
d. Fun
e. Tiring

20. What is the main idea of paragraph 3?

a. Linda Richards was not actually the first person to become a nurse.
b. Linda Richards became a nurse instead of becoming a missionary.
c. Linda Richards worked to make needed improvements to nursing.
d. Linda Richards wanted to teach nurses to read and write.

21. This question has two parts. After you answer Part A, answer Part B:

Part A: Which of the following conclusions is supported by this passage?

a. Nurses are not needed in hospitals and clinics.
b. Nurses will eventually replace doctors.
c. Nurses can help more people today than they could before.
d. Nurses will be required to study with more famous nurses.

Part B: Which of the following sentences from the passage supports the conclusion chosen in Part A?

a. She even went to England to study with Florence Nightingale, one of the most famous nurses in history.
b. Pretty soon, nurses who had an education in medicine were helping patients all over America.
c. These tasks are very important, but there is a lot more a nurse needs to know and do to help people get well.
d. Before long, all hospitals in America were keeping patient records.

22. What is the passage's main idea?

a. Linda Richards decided to become a nurse after caring for her mother.
b. Linda Richards invented a way for hospitals to keep better records.
c. Linda Richards was one of the first educated nurses in America.
d. Linda Richards worked hard to solve problems she saw in the field of nursing.

23. How did the author organize paragraph 4?

a. The author explains what caused Linda Richards to go to nursing school.
b. The author explains the events that happened at the beginning of Linda Richards's career.
c. The author explains how Linda Richards felt about being a nurse in Boston.
d. The author explains the problems in nursing that Linda Richards wanted to solve.

24. Why is paragraph 2 organized using a chronological pattern?

a. It describes the events that led Linda Richards to become a nurse.
b. It tells of the problem that Linda Richards wanted to solve as a nurse.
c. It explains the effects of Linda Richards becoming a nurse.
d. It shows why the reader should become a nurse.

25. Which sentence from the passage shows that Linda Richards helped others become better nurses?

a. Linda decided that she was going to become a nurse, not a missionary.
b. While she worked there, she invented a way of keeping records for each patient.
c. At these schools, she trained people in the modern methods of nursing.
d. Thanks to her, millions of people have lived longer and better lives.

Extended Response

Your STAAR test will include the following instructions for your extended response question. The response prompts used here are similar to the prompts you will see on the STAAR test.

26. Read the selection "Linda Richards: Medical Pioneer." Based on the information in the selection, write a response to the following:

Explain how Linda Richards's jobs at the hospitals helped her become a better nurse.

Write a well-organized informational essay that uses specific evidence from the selection to support your answer.

Remember to —

- clearly state your central idea
- organize your writing
- develop your ideas in detail
- use evidence from the selection in your response
- use correct spelling, capitalization, punctuation, and grammar

Manage your time carefully so that you can —

- review the selection
- plan your response
- write your response
- revise and edit your response

Revising

Courtney wrote the following paper about her class's field trip. Read the following paper and note the revisions that Courtney should make. Once you have read her paper, answer the questions that follow it.

Down on the Farm

(1) On the day of the field trip, our classroom was buzzing with excitement. (2) Finally, the time came to get on the bus. (3) I watched out the window as big buildings slipped by, then houses, and then fields. (4) The bus turned down a long, gravel driveway and stopped at the end next to a big red barn at the end of the driveway. (5) We were at the farm!

(6) We learned that Farmer Jones and his wife grew corn and pumpkins and raised cows and chickens. (7) First, we took a tour of the farm. (8) They had several farm workers to help take care of the farm. (9) Farmer Jones and his wife also had a small market where they sold their crops and some crops from other farmers who lived nearby.

(10) I loved walking through the cornfield with the dry stalks rustling above my head. (11) Farmer Jones also let me feed a calf from a bottle, and I loved feeling it suck and tug to get at the milk. (12) When we were done seeing the farm, Farmer Jones took us all to the market. (13) He took us to the market for some fresh corn on the cob. (14) It was so yummy!

(15) When the time came to get back on the bus, no one wanted to leave. (16) We thanked Farmer Jones and headed back to town. (17) I loved visiting the farm and seeing how Farmer Jones lived. (18) Maybe I will decide to be a farmer someday.

27. Part of sentence 4 needs to be removed because it is repetitive. What should be removed?

The bus turned down a long, gravel driveway and stopped at the end next to a big red barn at the end of the driveway.

a. The bus turned down
b. a long, gravel driveway
c. at the end next to a big red barn
d. at the end of the driveway

28. Which sentence is the best choice for the first sentence of paragraph 2?

a. Sentence 6
b. Sentence 7
c. Sentence 8
d. Sentence 9

29. Which of the following sentences shows the best way to combine sentences 12 and 13?

a. When we were done seeing the farm, we had fresh corn on the cob, and Farmer Jones took us all to the market.
b. Farmer Jones took us to the market for some fresh corn on the cob, and then we were done seeing the farm.
c. When we were done seeing the farm, Farmer Jones took us all to the market for some fresh corn on the cob.
d. For some fresh corn on the cob when we were done seeing the farm, Farmer Jones took us all to the market.

30. Which of the following sentences would be best to add after sentence 15?

a. It was time to get back on the bus.
b. We were not ready to say goodbye to Farmer Jones and all of his farm animals.
c. None of us wanted to ride the bus for our long journey back to town.
d. We were so tired from walking around all day.

Jacob wrote the following paper about the time his brother broke his arm. Read the following paper and note the revisions that Jacob should make. Once you have read his paper, answer the questions that follow it.

Some People Never Learn

(1) One lazy Sunday afternoon, all the boys in our neighborhood decided to play football in the big field on the corner. (2) There used to be a gas station there, but a construction company knocked it down. (3) My brother, Seth, went to play, so I went along to watch. (4) On the second play of the game, a big boy crashed into Seth and knocked him to the ground. (5) It had rained all morning, so the field was muddy and slick.

(6) I rushed over to Seth. (7) He was pale and shaking. (8) He was holding his arm. (9) He told me to run home and get Mom. (10) Mom came with the car, and we helped Seth get in and buckle his seatbelt. (11) Then we drove him to the hospital.

(12) In the emergency room, the doctors and nurses began working on Seth. (13) They sent him in for x-rays and gave him some pills to make the pain better. (14) Then, a doctor came in and said Seth broke his upper arm. (15) Seth's arm would have to be in a sling for six weeks to help it heal.

(16) For six long weeks, I helped Mom take care of Seth. (17) He needed help with almost everything. (18) Lucky for him, he didn't have to do chores for six weeks, and he even got to skip some of his schoolwork. (19) Finally, Seth's arm was better, and he could take off the sling. (20) The very next day, Seth was back out in the field playing football. (21) Some people never learn!

31. Which sentence does not belong in this essay?

a. Sentence 1
b. Sentence 2
c. Sentence 4
d. Sentence 10

32. Which of the following sentences should be moved to the very end of paragraph 1?

a. Sentence 1
b. Sentence 2
c. Sentence 3
d. Sentence 4

33. Sentences 7 and 8 can be combined. Please write one sentence that states the information given in sentences 7 and 8. Write the new sentence on the lines below.

____

____

____

Editing

Kate is writing an essay about how chocolate is made. Read the first two paragraphs of Kate's essay and look for errors that she needs to correct. Once you have read the paragraphs, answer the questions that follow them.

Where Does Chocolate Come From?

(1) People from around the world love chocolate, but do you know where it comes from? (2) You might be shocked to know that chocolate comes from a tree. (3) However, it is made from the seeds found in the fruit of the cacao tree. (4) Cacao trees grow in warm areas, such as the northern part of south america. (5) These seeds did not taste like the chocolate you can buy at the store. (6) The seeds, also called cacao, are very bitter. (7) The seeds go through a long process to become the sweet treat so many people enjoy.

(8) The first step in the process of making chocolate is to harvest and prepare the cacao seeds. (9) After the fruit of the cacao tree is harvestid, everything inside of it is left to ferment. (10) When a fruit ferments, it is left alone so that a chemical change can take place. (11) This process changes the way the seeds taste. (12) Once the fruit is fermented, the seeds are completely removed and dryed. (13) The seeds are then sent to people and companies that will use them in their own chocolate recipes.

34. Which change would correct the mistake in sentence 4?

a. Change *grow* to *grew.*
b. Change *in* to *on.*
c. Add a comma after *part.*
d. Change *south america* to *South America.*

35. Which change needs to be made to sentence 5?

a. Change *did* to *do.*
b. Change *taste* to *tastes.*
c. Change *at* to *for.*
d. No change is needed.

36. Which change would correct the mistake in sentence 9?

a. Add a comma after *After.*
b. Change *harvestid* to *harvested.*
c. Change *everything* to *every thing.*
d. Change *it* to *them.*

37. Choose the word that should replace *dryed* in sentence 12.

Once the fruit is fermented, the seeds are completely removed and ________.

driyed
driyd
dried
dride

Lance is writing an essay about gardening. Read the first two paragraphs of Lance's essay and look for errors that he needs to correct. Once you have read the paragraphs, answer the questions that follow them.

Going Gardening

(1) Growing a flower garden can be a fun and interesting activity. (2) Planting flower seeds and caring for the plant until it blooms allows you to watch up close to see how they grow. (3) However, not all flowers will grow well in any garden. (4) For example, each type need to be planted in the right type of soil and receive the right amount of water and sunlight in order to grow. (5) When planting a garden, it is important to research the type of flowers you want to grow so you can create a good environment for those flowers.

(6) Each species of flower grows best in a certain type of soil. (7) Flowers have roots and some flowers' roots need a lot of room to grow. (8) This means that the soil the seed is planted in should be loose enuph that the roots can grow as long as they need to. (9) Other flowers may have shortest roots that can't hold the plant up by themselves. (10) The seeds for these flowers should be planted in soil that stays tightly packed. (11) This soil will help the flower grow correctly because it can hold the roots and the bottom of the stem in place.

38. Which change would correct the mistake in sentence 4?

a. Change *example* to *exampel.*
b. Change *need* to *needs.*
c. Change *right* to *write.*
d. Change *grow* to *grew.*

39. Which change would correct the mistake in sentence 7?

a. Change *have* to *had.*
b. Add a comma before *and.*
c. Change *flowers'* to *flowers.*
d. Change *to* to *for.*

40. Which change would correct the mistake in sentence 8?

a. Change *is* to *are.*
b. Change *grow* to *grew.*
c. Change *enuph* to *enough.*
d. Change *they* to *them.*

41. Which change would correct the mistake in sentence 9?

a. Change *shortest* to *short.*
b. Change *can't* to *ca'nt.*
c. Change *hold* to *holds.*
d. Change *by* to *from.*

Answer Key and Explanations for Test #3

Reading

1. D: TEKS Standard (3.7)(C)

In line 11 of the poem, the speaker says that he or she would like to play. Throughout the poem, the speaker shows that he or she does not want to go to bed while others are still awake and doing things. This line tells the reader what the speaker would do if he or she did not have to go to bed, so choice D is correct. Line 2 describes what the speaker has to do during the wintertime. The speaker does not say he or she wants to do this, so choice A is incorrect. Line 6, choice B, shows something that is happening while the speaker should be going to sleep. It does not show that the speaker wants to get up and do something else, so choice B is incorrect. Line 9, choice C, shows that the speaker thinks going to bed at this time is difficult. However, it does not say that the speaker wants to do something else, so choice C is incorrect.

2. A: TEKS Standard (3.8)(A)

The speaker is young and needs to get plenty of sleep. Going to sleep early is good for the speaker. However, the speaker would rather do something fun, like get up and play. This shows the speaker disliking something that is good for him or her because it is not fun. The poem only says that the speaker must go to bed while the Sun is still up. It does not say the Sun never goes down, so choice B is incorrect. The poem shows that the grown-ups are still up when the speaker has to go to sleep. However, the poem does not show what life is like for the grown-ups. This makes choice C incorrect. The poem shows that the speaker must go to sleep early but does not want to. The poem does not say why the speaker is going to sleep at this time, so choice D is incorrect.

3. B: TEKS Standard (3.9)(B)

In stanza 2, the poem mentions birds hopping in the trees and grown-ups walking in the street. These events are happening while the speaker is going to bed, so choice B is correct. The poem does not show the speaker's dreams, since the speaker is awake throughout the poem. This makes choice A incorrect. The poem does not explain why the speaker must go to bed at this time, so choice C is incorrect. Stanza 3 gives the most information about why the speaker wants to stay up. It says that the speaker wants to play. It also shows that the speaker thinks it is hard to go to bed when the sky still looks like it does during the day, so choice D is incorrect.

4. C: TEKS Standard (3.6)(C)

The speaker says that he or she would rather play than go to bed. This means that the speaker will probably want to play when he or she wakes up the next day. This makes choice C the best choice. The speaker does not dislike the birds in the trees. The speaker just does not want to go to bed while the birds are still out. Choice A is unlikely, so it is incorrect. The poem does not show that the speaker has a hard time waking up. The speaker also shows that he or she prefers being up to going to bed. Choice B is unlikely, so it is incorrect. The speaker only complains about going to bed early. The speaker also does not show that he or she understands why it is good to go to bed early. Choice D is also unlikely, so it is incorrect.

5. C: TEKS Standard (3.10)(E)

The reader knows that the speaker wants to play and does not want to go to bed early. The reader also knows that the speaker sees the birds and hears the grown-ups walking. The reader can know the speaker's thoughts and feelings because the speaker is narrating the poem in the first person. The grown-ups' thoughts and feelings are not mentioned in the poem. This means that choices A and D are incorrect. The poem shows that the Sun is still out when the speaker has to go to bed. However, it does not state the time that the speaker goes to sleep. This makes Choice B incorrect.

6. B: TEKS Standard (3.8)(B)

The grown-ups are walking around and do not have to go to bed yet. The speaker is upset because he or she must go to bed. Since the speaker wants to be able to stay up like the grown-ups, the speaker is probably jealous of the grown-ups, so choice B is correct. The speaker does not observe how fast or slow the grown-ups are walking, so choice A is incorrect. The speaker is upset that he or she must go to bed while the grown-ups are awake. However, the poem does not show that the speaker is angry at the grown-ups, so choice C is incorrect. The speaker also does not share his or her thoughts about growing up, so choice D is incorrect.

7. B: TEKS Standard (3.6)(F)

In the story, Henry is quiet when Gloria is showing him to the judges. Maja, on the other hand, made lots of noise when Gloria showed her. In paragraph 8, Manuela thinks that the judges may take away points if an animal makes noise while it is being shown. Since Henry was quiet and Maja was noisy, Manuela thinks Henry will get a prize for his better behavior. This makes choice B correct. Both Maja and Henry looked healthy and well fed, so choice A is incorrect. Neither Manuela nor Gloria mentions that the judges may give points based on the goat's height or coat color, so choices C and D are incorrect.

8. C: TEKS Standard (3.8)(C)

Paragraph 7 describes what happens when Gloria shows Maja to the judges. Maja's behavior earns her a prize, which surprises Manuela, the narrator. This means that choice C is correct, since the events in paragraph 7 lead to Maja getting a prize, which causes Manuela's surprise. Maja's qualities are listed in paragraphs 3 and 4, so choice A is incorrect. Paragraph 6 tells what the goats are expected to do in the ring, so choice B is incorrect. Manuela is surprised that Maja received a better reward than Henry, but she is not disappointed. This means that choice D is incorrect.

9. C: TEKS Standard (3.7)(D)

Paragraphs 7 and 8 tell what happened when Gloria showed Maja and Henry in the ring. Both goats obeyed Gloria. However, Maja made noise as she followed Gloria, and Henry did not. This matches the summary in choice C, so choice C is the correct answer. Maja did not run away from Gloria, so choice A is incorrect. The goats did not tie for second place. Also, the prizes the goats received are mentioned in paragraphs 9 and 10, not 7 and 8. These points make Choice B incorrect. Neither of Gloria's goats are disqualified, and Henry followed Gloria silently. This means choice D is incorrect.

10. B: TEKS Standard (3.9)(A)

This play teaches the lesson that you should always do your best, even when you think you will fail. Fables are short, fictional stories that usually teach a lesson, so choice B is correct. There are no talking animals in this story, so choice A is incorrect. Fables may have more than one main character. This story also has more than one main character, so choice C is incorrect. Many fables have happy endings. An unhappy ending is not a characteristic of a fable, so choice D is incorrect.

11. C: TEKS Standard (3.9)(C)

When Savannah finishes her audition, she walks out of the door and sits down next to Bailey. Then, Mr. Dawn also walks through the door. After Daniel goes in for his audition, and some time passes, these same events are described in this stage direction. This shows that Daniel has probably completed his audition, making choice C correct. This stage direction does not show any actions that suggest Daniel is nervous, so choice A is incorrect. The students learn whether or not they made the choir by looking at a list of names. This stage direction does not show Daniel after he has looked at the list, so choice B is incorrect. The passage does not show whether or not the students brought their music to the audition, so choice D is incorrect.

12. B: TEKS Standard (3.3)(C)

In scene 4, Bailey explains that she got nervous and did not sing during her audition. She says she wishes she had tried to sing again after she messed up. This shows that she regrets that she did not sing. This shows that *disappointed* means that Bailey is upset about what she did. This means that *disappointed* means the same as *let down,* so choice B is correct. Bailey does not yell, say mean things, or do anything else that would show that she is angry, so choice A is incorrect. Bailey is upset about her actions, so she would not be excited or proud when she says this line. This means choices C and D are incorrect.

13. C: TEKS Standard (3.10)(C)

The box titled "Cast of Characters" gives the reader more information about how old each character is and what they might do in the story. For example, this box shows that Savannah, Bailey, and Daniel are all children and students, and that Mr. Dawn is an adult teacher. This shows that Savannah, Bailey, and Daniel will likely need to listen to Mr. Dawn, or that Mr. Dawn will lead or give the students instructions. This information shows what role each character may have in the story, so choice C is correct. The information in the box does not explain the setting, so it would not help the reader understand what the characters would wear. This makes Choice A incorrect. The information in the box does not describe or give clues about the characters' voices or their skills, so choices B and D are incorrect.

14. C: TEKS Standard (3.6)(E)

In "The State Fair of Texas," Maja made noise when she was being shown. Because of this, Manuela was surprised that she won second place. In "Do Your Best," Savannah made mistakes during her choir audition. Because of this, she was surprised when she was chosen to be in the choir. Both Manuela and Savannah were surprised, so choice C is correct. Manuela did not go to an audition in "The State Fair of Texas," so choice A is incorrect. Manuela also did not show goats. Instead, she watched her cousin show goats, so choice B is incorrect. In "Do Your Best," Savannah sang for an audition. She did not show goats, so choice D is incorrect.

15. D: TEKS Standard (3.6)(E)

In "The State Fair of Texas," when Maja began bleating, Gloria continued showing her. She did not give up just because Maja was noisy. In "Do Your Best," Bailey made a mistake at the beginning of her audition. Since she was nervous and messed up right away, she gave up. This means that choice D is correct. In "The State Fair of Texas," Gloria showed goats, and in "Do Your Best," Bailey went to an audition. This is the opposite of what choice A says, so it is incorrect. In "The State Fair of Texas," Gloria's goats both receive an award. She is rewarded for her hard work. In "Do Your Best," Bailey does not make the choir, so she is not rewarded. This makes Choice B incorrect. Paragraphs 2 and 4 of "The State Fair of Texas" show that Gloria took care of Maja and Henry and prepared them to be shown at the fair. This means that choice C is incorrect.

16. A: TEKS Standard (3.6)(E)

In "The State Fair of Texas," Manuela does not expect Maja to earn a high ranking, because she was noisy. However, Maja comes in second place. In "Do Your Best," Savannah does not expect to earn a spot in the choir because she made mistakes during her audition. However, she does make the choir. These events support the idea that things may turn out better than you expect them to. In "Do Your Best," Mr. Dawn tells Bailey that she will have another chance to audition next year. However, the story "The State Fair of Texas" does not mention second chances, so choice B is incorrect. In "Do Your Best," Bailey and Savannah practice, but they still make mistakes. However, "The State Fair of Texas" does not describe how much Gloria practiced with her goats, so choice C is incorrect. In "Do Your Best," multiple characters experience stage fright. However, none of the characters in "The State Fair of Texas" mention stage fright, so choice D is incorrect.

17. B: TEKS Standard (3.3)(D)

The passage title calls Linda Richards a *pioneer*. The central idea of the passage is how Linda Richards tried new things that improved nursing. It even tells how she invented a new way for hospitals to keep records. This shows that Linda Richards was an *inventor*. This is a synonym of *pioneer*, so choice B is correct. Linda Richards did not simply follow what others did. She chose her own career and looked for new and better ways to help patients. She was not a follower, so choice A is incorrect. Linda Richards lived in a few places and traveled to England to learn from Florence Nightingale. However, the central idea of the passage is not that she was a traveler, so choice C is incorrect. The passage says that Linda Richards cared for patients but does not say that she was a patient. This means choice D is incorrect.

18. D: TEKS Standard (3.3)(A)

Paragraph 4 says that, before Linda Richards's invention, hospitals did not keep good track of patients and their health. Patient records were used to solve this problem. This means that records must help people keep track of information. One way to do this is to write down or type information so it can be read later. This matches Definition 4, so choice D is the correct answer. Paragraph 4 does not mention music or being entertained, so choices A and B are incorrect. The hospital did not need to compare how well different patients performed tasks or feats, so choice C is incorrect.

19. C, E: TEKS Standard (3.6)(F)

Paragraph 4 describes Linda Richards's experience at her first hospital job. The passage says that the nurses were not trained, and they had to work for most of the day. They also did not always get enough sleep, because they had to wake up to take care of patients. The nurses were expected to do lots of hard work with little rest. These conditions were harsh and tiring. Choices C and E are correct. *Pleasant*, *enjoyable*, and *fun* would be used to describe good conditions. Since the conditions were not good, choices A, B, and D are incorrect.

20. C: TEKS Standard (3.6)(G)

Paragraph 3 explains that, before Linda Richards's lifetime, nurses could not do much to help their patients. The paragraph ends by saying that Linda Richards helped fix this problem. Linda Richards helped make needed changes that improved nursing, so choice C is correct. Choice A says Linda Richards was not the first nurse. This is just a detail from the paragraph. It is not what the paragraph is about, so choice A is incorrect. Linda Richards's decision to become a nurse instead of a missionary is only mentioned in paragraph 2. This makes Choice B incorrect. The passage does not say that Linda Richards tried to teach anyone to read or write, meaning Choice D is incorrect.

21. TEKS Standard (3.6)(H)

Part A: C: Because of Linda Richards's efforts and accomplishments, there are more nurses. These nurses can help more patients. This means that choice C is correct. The passage says that nurses can do more, not that they are no longer needed in hospitals and clinics. Choice A is incorrect. The passage does not say that nurses can now do all that doctors can do, so choice B is incorrect. While Linda Richards learned from Florence Nightingale, a famous nurse, the passage does not say that other nurses must learn from famous nurses. This means choice D is incorrect.

Part B: B: The sentence in choice B shows the effect of Linda Richards teaching people how to be better nurses. The sentence says that educated nurses were helping patients throughout the country. This means that nurses were then able to help more patients than they could before. This supports the conclusion that today's nurses can help more people than the first nurses could. Choice B is the correct answer. Choice A shows that Linda Richards received training from a famous nurse. Choice C shows that nurses in the past did not have the education they needed to help many people heal. Choice D shows that Linda Richards invented something that helped hospitals keep better records. None of the details in choices A, C, and D show that today's nurses can help more people than they could before.

22. D: TEKS Standard (3.9)(Di)

The passage explains how Linda Richards became a nurse, saw that there were problems in nursing, and worked to learn more so she could help improve nursing. This means that choice D is correct. Caring for her mother was what inspired Linda Richards to become a nurse. During her early career, she invented a better record-keeping method. She was also one of the first nurses in America to go to nursing school. While all of these are facts mentioned in the passage, they are supporting details. Each of these facts is only mentioned once or twice. None of these ideas are the central idea of the passage, so choices A, B, and C are incorrect.

23. B: TEKS Standard (3.9)(Diii)

Paragraph 4 tells the reader about Linda Richards's first job, her choice to go to nursing school, her first job after she graduated, and her success in inventing a new method of keeping records. These are all events that happened at the beginning of Linda Richards's career as a nurse. Choice B is, therefore, correct. The paragraph talks about events that happened after Linda Richards went to nursing school. This means that the paragraph was not written to show why she went to school, making choice A incorrect. Linda Richards's feelings and thoughts are not described in this paragraph, so choice C is also incorrect. The paragraph mentions that Linda Richards invented a better way to keep patient records. However, the rest of the paragraph talks about events, not problems in nursing, so choice D is incorrect.

24. A: TEKS Standard (3.10)(B)

Paragraph 2 tells the reader some events that happened during Linda Richards's childhood. One of these events is the death of her father. Linda Richards's father wanted her to become a missionary. However, he was no longer alive to tell her to become a missionary instead of a nurse. Another event was her mother becoming sick. Linda Richards took care of her mother, and this experience made her want to become a nurse. These events caused Linda Richards to become a nurse, so choice A is correct. Linda Richards did not know about the problems in nursing until after these events, so choice B is incorrect. The effects of Linda Richards's career as a nurse also occurred after these events, so choice C is incorrect. This paragraph simply describes events that happened. It does not tell the reader reasons why it is good to become a nurse, so choice D is incorrect.

25. C: TEKS Standard (3.7)(C)

The sentence in choice C shows that Linda Richards taught others new methods for nursing. By doing this, she helped others become better nurses, so choice C is correct. The event in choice A occurred before Linda Richards began teaching other nurses, so choice A is incorrect. The sentence in choice B describes Linda Richards's invention. This invention helped doctors, nurses, and patients. However, it did not show others how to become better nurses, so choice B is incorrect. The sentence in choice D shows that Linda Richards's actions have helped millions of patients. Since this sentence shows that she helped patients instead of how she helped nurses, choice D is incorrect.

Extended Response

25. TEKS Standard (3.12)(B)

Please use the rubric below to make sure your response meets these common criteria. Try to have a friend or family member grade your response for you or take a break after writing your response and return to grade it yourself with fresh eyes.

Below is an excerpt of the STAAR Grades 3-5 Informational Writing Rubric.

<table>
<tr><th>Score Point</th><th>Organization and Development of Ideas</th></tr>
<tr><td>3</td><td><ul><li>Central idea is clear and fully developed
The central idea is clearly identifiable. The focus is consistent throughout, creating a response that is unified and easy to follow.</li><li>Organization is effective
A purposeful structure that includes an effective introduction and conclusion is evident. The organizational structure is appropriate and effectively supports the development of the central idea. The sentences, paragraphs, or ideas are logically connected in purposeful and highly effective ways.</li><li>Evidence is specific, well chosen, and relevant
The response includes relevant text-based evidence that is clearly explained and consistently supports and develops the central idea. For pairs in grades 3-5, evidence is drawn from at least one text. The response reflects a thorough understanding of the writing purpose.</li><li>Expression of ideas is clear and effective
The writer's word choice is specific, purposeful, and enhances the response. Almost all sentences and phrases are effectively crafted to convey the writer's ideas and contribute to the overall quality of the response and the clarity of the message.</li></ul></td></tr>
<tr><th>Score Point</th><th>Conventions</th></tr>
<tr><td>2</td><td>Student writing demonstrates consistent command of grade-level-appropriate conventions, including correct:<ul><li>sentence construction</li><li>punctuation</li><li>capitalization</li><li>grammar</li><li>spelling</li></ul>The response has few errors, but those errors do not impact the clarity of the writing.</td></tr>
</table>

Revising

27. D: TEKS Standard (3.11)(C)

The original sentence tells the reader twice that the bus stopped at the end of the driveway. The words in choice C show the reader that the bus stopped at the end of the driveway and that it stopped next to a red barn. The portion of the sentence in choice D only tells the reader that the bus stopped at the end of the driveway. Since the words in choice C give the reader more information, they should stay in the sentence. The words in choice D should be removed from the sentence, so choice D is the correct answer. If the words in choice A were removed, the sentence would not make sense. If the words in choice B were removed, the reader would not know what kind of driveway the bus traveled down. There would also still be repeated information in the sentence.

28. B: TEKS Standard (3.11)(Bi)

Sentence 7 is the best choice because it clearly shows the overall topic of the paragraph. This is what the first sentence of a paragraph should do. Sentences 6, 8, and 9 all describe what the students learned during their tour of the farm. Using sentence 6, 8, or 9 as the first sentence of the paragraph would not show the reader that the paragraph is about what the students learned on the tour. Using one of these sentences would make it seem like the paragraph is all about just one of the things they learned. Choices A, C, and D are incorrect.

29. C: TEKS Standard (3.11)(C)

When two sentences are combined, the new sentence should have the same meaning as the two original sentences. The new sentence should also be clear and use proper grammar. Choice C is a complete sentence, uses correct grammar, and has the same meaning as sentences 12 and 13. Choice A is incorrect because it has a different meaning. Choice A says that the students ate corn on the cob before they went to the market. Choice B also has a different meaning than the original sentences. Choice B says that the students ate corn and visited the market before they finished seeing the farm. Choice D is incorrect because it is unclear and difficult to understand.

30. B: TEKS Standard (3.11)(Bii)

Choice B states that the students did not want to leave Farmer Jones and the animals. This sentence makes sense and fits in this paragraph, so choice B is correct. Choice A is incorrect because it repeats the information that was given in sentence 15. Choices C is incorrect because there are no details that suggest that the students dislike riding the bus. Choice D is incorrect because it does not make sense in this paragraph. Sentence 15 says that the students did not want to get on the bus to leave. Choice D would be a reason that the students would want to get back on the bus.

31. B: TEKS Standard (3.11)(Bii)

Sentence 2 gives details that do not help the reader understand the events in the story. These details distract the reader from the story, so choice B is correct. Choices A, C, and D are incorrect because sentences 1, 4, and 10 all give details that help the reader understand the story.

32. D: TEKS Standard (3.11)(Bi)

Moving sentence 4 to the end of paragraph 1 would make the paragraph clearer. Sentence 5 gives details that help the reader understand the cause of the events described in sentence 4, so it should come first. Choice A is incorrect because sentence 1 is the introductory sentence of the story, so it must come first. Choice B is incorrect because sentence 2 would not make sense at the end of this paragraph. Choice C is incorrect because the events in sentence 3 come before the events in sentence 4. If sentence 3 were moved to the end of the paragraph, the events would be out of order.

33. TEKS Standard (3.11)(C)

Sentence 7 says that Seth was pale and shaking, and sentence 8 says that he was holding his arm. A sentence that correctly combines these sentences should include the details from both sentences. It should also make sense and be grammatically correct. An example of a sentence that correctly combines sentences 7 and 8 is: "He was pale and shaking, and he was holding his arm."

Editing

34. D: TEKS Standard (3.11)(Dix)

South America is a place, so it is a proper noun. This means that *south america* should be changed to *South America*. Choice D is the correct change. Choice A is incorrect because the sentence is in present tense, but *grew* is a past tense word. Cacao trees grow in certain areas, not on those areas, so choice B is incorrect. Commas are usually added after prepositional phrases. However, they do not always need to be added before prepositional phrases, so choice C is incorrect.

35. A: TEKS Standard (3.11)(Dii)

Sentence 5 is in the present tense, but *did* is a past tense verb. *Did* should be changed to *do*, which is a present tense verb. Choice A is correct. *Seeds* is a plural noun, so it should be used with a plural verb. *Tastes* is a singular verb, so choice B is incorrect. The preposition *at* is used to show someone or something's location. This preposition is used correctly in sentence 5, so choice C is incorrect. Since *did* should be changed to *do* in this sentence, choice D is incorrect.

36. B: TEKS Standard (3.2)(Bv)

The word *harvested* is the past tense version of the verb *harvest*. Adding the suffix *-ed* changes a present tense verb to a past tense verb. This means that *harvestid* is misspelled, and choice B is correct. A comma is usually added after a prepositional phrase. They are not added after prepositions that are by themselves. *After* is just a preposition, so it should not be followed by a comma. This makes choice A incorrect. *Everything* is spelled correctly because it is a compound word. This means choice C is incorrect. When talking about an object, *it* is a singular pronoun, and *them* is a plural pronoun. The word *the* shows that *fruit* is singular, so the word *it* should be used as its pronoun, making choice D incorrect.

37. dried: TEKS Standard (3.2)(Bvii)

The word *dried* is the past tense version of the word *dry*. *Dried* is a combination of *dry* and the suffix *-ed*. Adding the suffix *-ed* changes a present tense verb to a past tense verb. When adding a suffix to a word that ends in *y*, the *y* is usually changed to *ie*. The spellings *driyed*, *driyd*, and *dride* are not examples of how a word ending in *y* should be spelled when a suffix is added to it.

38. B: TEKS Standard (3.11)(Di)

The word *each* shows that *type* is a singular noun. Singular nouns should be used with singular verbs. *Need* is a plural verb, so it should be changed to the singular verb *needs*. This means choice B is correct. The word *example* is spelled correctly in the passage, so choice A is incorrect. *Right* and *write* are homophones. *Right* means something is correct, while *write* means that someone is drawing letters. The word *right* is used correctly in the sentence, so choice C is incorrect. This sentence is in the present tense, so it should use present tense verbs. *Grow* is a present tense verb, and *grew* is a past tense verb, so choice D is incorrect.

39. B: TEKS Standard (3.11)(Dx)

Sentence 7 has two independent clauses, so it is a compound sentence. In a compound sentence, the two clauses are usually connected by a comma and a coordinating conjunction. There is no comma in sentence 7. A comma should be added before *and*, so choice B is correct. Sentence 7 is in the present tense, so it should contain present tense verbs. *Have* is a present tense verb, and *had* is a past tense verb. This means choice A is incorrect. Sentence 7 talks about the roots that belong to some flowers. The apostrophe in *flowers'* is used to show that the flowers have, or possess, the roots. This makes choice C incorrect. The preposition *to* is sometimes used to show the purpose or reason for something. Choice D is incorrect because *to* is used correctly to show that the roots need room because they need to grow.

40. C: TEKS Standard (3.2)(Bi)

Enuph is a misspelled version of the word *enough,* so choice C is correct. The word *enough* uses the vowel team *ou* and the consonant team *gh*. Soil is a singular noun, so it must be used with a singular verb. The verb *is* is a singular verb, so it is the correct verb. Using *are* would be incorrect because it is a plural verb, so choice A is incorrect. The sentence is in present tense, so it should use present tense verbs. *Grow* is a present tense verb, and *grew* is a past tense verb. The correct verb to use is *grow*, so choice B is incorrect. The pronoun *they* is used as the subject of a sentence. The pronoun *them* is used as the object of a sentence. In sentence 8, the word *they* comes before the words *need to*. *They* is used in place of *roots*. Since the roots are doing the action, which is *needing*, the roots are the subject. This means that *they* is the correct pronoun to use in place of *roots*, and choice D is incorrect.

41. A: TEKS Standard (3.11)(Div)

Adjectives that end in *-est* are used for comparing more than two things. Adjectives that end in *-er* are usually used to compare two things. Adjectives that do not end in these suffixes are just meant to describe things. In sentence 9, the roots are being described, but they are not being compared to anything. This means that the correct adjective to use is *short*, not *shortest*, making choice A correct. When using apostrophes in contractions, the apostrophe should go where letters have been taken out. *Can't* is a contraction of *cannot*. The *o* and one of the *n*'s is removed, so the apostrophe should go between *n* and *t*. This makes choice B incorrect. *Flowers* is a plural noun, so it should be used with a plural verb. *Hold* is a plural verb, and *holds* is a singular verb, so choice C is incorrect. *From* is used to show that something is moving in the opposite direction as something else. *From* does not make sense in place of *by* in sentence 9, so choice D is incorrect.

How to Overcome Test Anxiety

Just the thought of taking a test is enough to make most people a little nervous. A test is an important event that can have a long-term impact on your future, so it's important to take it seriously and it's natural to feel anxious about performing well. But just because anxiety is normal, that doesn't mean that it's helpful in test taking, or that you should simply accept it as part of your life. Anxiety can have a variety of effects. These effects can be mild, like making you feel slightly nervous, or severe, like blocking your ability to focus or remember even a simple detail.

If you experience test anxiety—whether severe or mild—it's important to know how to beat it. To discover this, first you need to understand what causes test anxiety.

Causes of Test Anxiety

While we often think of anxiety as an uncontrollable emotional state, it can actually be caused by simple, practical things. One of the most common causes of test anxiety is that a person does not feel adequately prepared for their test. This feeling can be the result of many different issues such as poor study habits or lack of organization, but the most common culprit is time management. Starting to study too late, failing to organize your study time to cover all of the material, or being distracted while you study will mean that you're not well prepared for the test. This may lead to cramming the night before, which will cause you to be physically and mentally exhausted for the test. Poor time management also contributes to feelings of stress, fear, and hopelessness as you realize you are not well prepared but don't know what to do about it.

Other times, test anxiety is not related to your preparation for the test but comes from unresolved fear. This may be a past failure on a test, or poor performance on tests in general. It may come from comparing yourself to others who seem to be performing better or from the stress of living up to expectations. Anxiety may be driven by fears of the future—how failure on this test would affect your educational and career goals. These fears are often completely irrational, but they can still negatively impact your test performance.

Elements of Test Anxiety

As mentioned earlier, test anxiety is considered to be an emotional state, but it has physical and mental components as well. Sometimes you may not even realize that you are suffering from test anxiety until you notice the physical symptoms. These can include trembling hands, rapid heartbeat, sweating, nausea, and tense muscles. Extreme anxiety may lead to fainting or vomiting. Obviously, any of these symptoms can have a negative impact on testing. It is important to recognize them as soon as they begin to occur so that you can address the problem before it damages your performance.

The mental components of test anxiety include trouble focusing and inability to remember learned information. During a test, your mind is on high alert, which can help you recall information and stay focused for an extended period of time. However, anxiety interferes with your mind's natural processes, causing you to blank out, even on the questions you know well. The strain of testing during anxiety makes it difficult to stay focused, especially on a test that may take several hours. Extreme anxiety can take a huge mental toll, making it difficult not only to recall test information but even to understand the test questions or pull your thoughts together.

Effects of Test Anxiety

Test anxiety is like a disease—if left untreated, it will get progressively worse. Anxiety leads to poor performance, and this reinforces the feelings of fear and failure, which in turn lead to poor performances on subsequent tests. It can grow from a mild nervousness to a crippling condition. If allowed to progress, test anxiety can have a big impact on your schooling, and consequently on your future.

Test anxiety can spread to other parts of your life. Anxiety on tests can become anxiety in any stressful situation, and blanking on a test can turn into panicking in a job situation. But fortunately, you don't have to let anxiety rule your testing and determine your grades. There are a number of relatively simple steps you can take to move past anxiety and function normally on a test and in the rest of life.

Physical Steps for Beating Test Anxiety

While test anxiety is a serious problem, the good news is that it can be overcome. It doesn't have to control your ability to think and remember information. While it may take time, you can begin taking steps today to beat anxiety.

Just as your first hint that you may be struggling with anxiety comes from the physical symptoms, the first step to treating it is also physical. Rest is crucial for having a clear, strong mind. If you are tired, it is much easier to give in to anxiety. But if you establish good sleep habits, your body and mind will be ready to perform optimally, without the strain of exhaustion. Additionally, sleeping well helps you to retain information better, so you're more likely to recall the answers when you see the test questions.

Getting good sleep means more than going to bed on time. It's important to allow your brain time to relax. Take study breaks from time to time so it doesn't get overworked, and don't study right before bed. Take time to rest your mind before trying to rest your body, or you may find it difficult to fall asleep.

Along with sleep, other aspects of physical health are important in preparing for a test. Good nutrition is vital for good brain function. Sugary foods and drinks may give a burst of energy but this burst is followed by a crash, both physically and emotionally. Instead, fuel your body with protein and vitamin-rich foods.

Also, drink plenty of water. Dehydration can lead to headaches and exhaustion, especially if your brain is already under stress from the rigors of the test. Particularly if your test is a long one, drink water during the breaks. And if possible, take an energy-boosting snack to eat between sections.

Along with sleep and diet, a third important part of physical health is exercise. Maintaining a steady workout schedule is helpful, but even taking 5-minute study breaks to walk can help get your blood pumping faster and clear your head. Exercise also releases endorphins, which contribute to a positive feeling and can help combat test anxiety.

When you nurture your physical health, you are also contributing to your mental health. If your body is healthy, your mind is much more likely to be healthy as well. So take time to rest, nourish your body with healthy food and water, and get moving as much as possible. Taking these physical steps will make you stronger and more able to take the mental steps necessary to overcome test anxiety.

Mental Steps for Beating Test Anxiety

Working on the mental side of test anxiety can be more challenging, but as with the physical side, there are clear steps you can take to overcome it. As mentioned earlier, test anxiety often stems from lack of preparation, so the obvious solution is to prepare for the test. Effective studying may be the most important weapon you have for beating test anxiety, but you can and should employ several other mental tools to combat fear.

First, boost your confidence by reminding yourself of past success—tests or projects that you aced. If you're putting as much effort into preparing for this test as you did for those, there's no reason you should expect to fail here. Work hard to prepare; then trust your preparation.

Second, surround yourself with encouraging people. It can be helpful to find a study group, but be sure that the people you're around will encourage a positive attitude. If you spend time with others who are anxious or cynical, this will only contribute to your own anxiety. Look for others who are motivated to study hard from a desire to succeed, not from a fear of failure.

Third, reward yourself. A test is physically and mentally tiring, even without anxiety, and it can be helpful to have something to look forward to. Plan an activity following the test, regardless of the outcome, such as going to a movie or getting ice cream.

When you are taking the test, if you find yourself beginning to feel anxious, remind yourself that you know the material. Visualize successfully completing the test. Then take a few deep, relaxing breaths and return to it. Work through the questions carefully but with confidence, knowing that you are capable of succeeding.

Developing a healthy mental approach to test taking will also aid in other areas of life. Test anxiety affects more than just the actual test—it can be damaging to your mental health and even contribute to depression. It's important to beat test anxiety before it becomes a problem for more than testing.

Study Strategy

Being prepared for the test is necessary to combat anxiety, but what does being prepared look like? You may study for hours on end and still not feel prepared. What you need is a strategy for test prep. The next few pages outline our recommended steps to help you plan out and conquer the challenge of preparation.

Step 1: Scope Out the Test

Learn everything you can about the format (multiple choice, essay, etc.) and what will be on the test. Gather any study materials, course outlines, or sample exams that may be available. Not only will this help you to prepare, but knowing what to expect can help to alleviate test anxiety.

Step 2: Map Out the Material

Look through the textbook or study guide and make note of how many chapters or sections it has. Then divide these over the time you have. For example, if a book has 15 chapters and you have five days to study, you need to cover three chapters each day. Even better, if you have the time, leave an extra day at the end for overall review after you have gone through the material in depth.

If time is limited, you may need to prioritize the material. Look through it and make note of which sections you think you already have a good grasp on, and which need review. While you are studying, skim quickly through the familiar sections and take more time on the challenging parts.

Write out your plan so you don't get lost as you go. Having a written plan also helps you feel more in control of the study, so anxiety is less likely to arise from feeling overwhelmed at the amount to cover.

STEP 3: GATHER YOUR TOOLS

Decide what study method works best for you. Do you prefer to highlight in the book as you study and then go back over the highlighted portions? Or do you type out notes of the important information? Or is it helpful to make flashcards that you can carry with you? Assemble the pens, index cards, highlighters, post-it notes, and any other materials you may need so you won't be distracted by getting up to find things while you study.

If you're having a hard time retaining the information or organizing your notes, experiment with different methods. For example, try color-coding by subject with colored pens, highlighters, or post-it notes. If you learn better by hearing, try recording yourself reading your notes so you can listen while in the car, working out, or simply sitting at your desk. Ask a friend to quiz you from your flashcards, or try teaching someone the material to solidify it in your mind.

STEP 4: CREATE YOUR ENVIRONMENT

It's important to avoid distractions while you study. This includes both the obvious distractions like visitors and the subtle distractions like an uncomfortable chair (or a too-comfortable couch that makes you want to fall asleep). Set up the best study environment possible: good lighting and a comfortable work area. If background music helps you focus, you may want to turn it on, but otherwise keep the room quiet. If you are using a computer to take notes, be sure you don't have any other windows open, especially applications like social media, games, or anything else that could distract you. Silence your phone and turn off notifications. Be sure to keep water close by so you stay hydrated while you study (but avoid unhealthy drinks and snacks).

Also, take into account the best time of day to study. Are you freshest first thing in the morning? Try to set aside some time then to work through the material. Is your mind clearer in the afternoon or evening? Schedule your study session then. Another method is to study at the same time of day that you will take the test, so that your brain gets used to working on the material at that time and will be ready to focus at test time.

STEP 5: STUDY!

Once you have done all the study preparation, it's time to settle into the actual studying. Sit down, take a few moments to settle your mind so you can focus, and begin to follow your study plan. Don't give in to distractions or let yourself procrastinate. This is your time to prepare so you'll be ready to fearlessly approach the test. Make the most of the time and stay focused.

Of course, you don't want to burn out. If you study too long you may find that you're not retaining the information very well. Take regular study breaks. For example, taking five minutes out of every hour to walk briskly, breathing deeply and swinging your arms, can help your mind stay fresh.

As you get to the end of each chapter or section, it's a good idea to do a quick review. Remind yourself of what you learned and work on any difficult parts. When you feel that you've mastered the material, move on to the next part. At the end of your study session, briefly skim through your notes again.

But while review is helpful, cramming last minute is NOT. If at all possible, work ahead so that you won't need to fit all your study into the last day. Cramming overloads your brain with more information than it can process and retain, and your tired mind may struggle to recall even previously learned information when it is overwhelmed with last-minute study. Also, the urgent nature of cramming and the stress placed on your brain contribute to anxiety. You'll be more likely to go to the test feeling unprepared and having trouble thinking clearly.

So don't cram, and don't stay up late before the test, even just to review your notes at a leisurely pace. Your brain needs rest more than it needs to go over the information again. In fact, plan to finish your studies by noon or early afternoon the day before the test. Give your brain the rest of the day to relax or focus on other things, and get a good night's sleep. Then you will be fresh for the test and better able to recall what you've studied.

Step 6: Take a Practice Test

Many courses offer sample tests, either online or in the study materials. This is an excellent resource to check whether you have mastered the material, as well as to prepare for the test format and environment.

Check the test format ahead of time: the number of questions, the type (multiple choice, free response, etc.), and the time limit. Then create a plan for working through them. For example, if you have 30 minutes to take a 60-question test, your limit is 30 seconds per question. Spend less time on the questions you know well so that you can take more time on the difficult ones.

If you have time to take several practice tests, take the first one open book, with no time limit. Work through the questions at your own pace and make sure you fully understand them. Gradually work up to taking a test under test conditions: sit at a desk with all study materials put away and set a timer. Pace yourself to make sure you finish the test with time to spare and go back to check your answers if you have time.

After each test, check your answers. On the questions you missed, be sure you understand why you missed them. Did you misread the question (tests can use tricky wording)? Did you forget the information? Or was it something you hadn't learned? Go back and study any shaky areas that the practice tests reveal.

Taking these tests not only helps with your grade, but also aids in combating test anxiety. If you're already used to the test conditions, you're less likely to worry about it, and working through tests until you're scoring well gives you a confidence boost. Go through the practice tests until you feel comfortable, and then you can go into the test knowing that you're ready for it.

Test Tips

On test day, you should be confident, knowing that you've prepared well and are ready to answer the questions. But aside from preparation, there are several test day strategies you can employ to maximize your performance.

First, as stated before, get a good night's sleep the night before the test (and for several nights before that, if possible). Go into the test with a fresh, alert mind rather than staying up late to study.

Try not to change too much about your normal routine on the day of the test. It's important to eat a nutritious breakfast, but if you normally don't eat breakfast at all, consider eating just a protein bar. If you're a coffee drinker, go ahead and have your normal coffee. Just make sure you time it so that the caffeine doesn't wear off right in the middle of your test. Avoid sugary beverages, and drink enough water to stay hydrated but not so much that you need a restroom break 10 minutes into the test. If your test isn't first thing in the morning, consider going for a walk or doing a light workout before the test to get your blood flowing.

Allow yourself enough time to get ready, and leave for the test with plenty of time to spare so you won't have the anxiety of scrambling to arrive in time. Another reason to be early is to select a good seat. It's helpful to sit away from doors and windows, which can be distracting. Find a good seat, get out your supplies, and settle your mind before the test begins.

When the test begins, start by going over the instructions carefully, even if you already know what to expect. Make sure you avoid any careless mistakes by following the directions.

Then begin working through the questions, pacing yourself as you've practiced. If you're not sure on an answer, don't spend too much time on it, and don't let it shake your confidence. Either skip it and come back later, or eliminate as many wrong answers as possible and guess among the remaining ones. Don't dwell on these questions as you continue—put them out of your mind and focus on what lies ahead.

Be sure to read all of the answer choices, even if you're sure the first one is the right answer. Sometimes you'll find a better one if you keep reading. But don't second-guess yourself if you do immediately know the answer. Your gut instinct is usually right. Don't let test anxiety rob you of the information you know.

If you have time at the end of the test (and if the test format allows), go back and review your answers. Be cautious about changing any, since your first instinct tends to be correct, but make sure you didn't misread any of the questions or accidentally mark the wrong answer choice. Look over any you skipped and make an educated guess.

At the end, leave the test feeling confident. You've done your best, so don't waste time worrying about your performance or wishing you could change anything. Instead, celebrate the successful completion of this test. And finally, use this test to learn how to deal with anxiety even better next time.

Review Video: Test Anxiety
Visit mometrix.com/academy and enter code: 100340

Important Qualification

Not all anxiety is created equal. If your test anxiety is causing major issues in your life beyond the classroom or testing center, or if you are experiencing troubling physical symptoms related to your anxiety, it may be a sign of a serious physiological or psychological condition. If this sounds like your situation, we strongly encourage you to seek professional help.

Online Resources

Due to our efforts to try to keep this book to a manageable length, we've created a link that will give you access to all of your online resources:

mometrix.com/resources719/staarg3rla

It's Your Moment, Let's Celebrate It!

Share your story @mometrixtestpreparation